DISCARD

Powerboating

Powerboating

Your First Book for Your First Boat

Captain Ken Kreisler

SEAHORSE PUBLISHING

Seahorse Publishing books may be purchased in bulk at special discounts for sales promotion, corporate gifts, fund-raising, or educational purposes. Special editions can also be created to specifications. For details, contact the Special Sales Department, Skyhorse Publishing, 307 West 36th Street, 11th Floor, New York, NY 10018 or info@skyhorsepublishing.com.

Seahorse® and Skyhorse Publishing® are registered trademarks of Skyhorse Publishing, Inc.®, a Delaware corporation.

Visit our website at www.skyhorsepublishing.com.

10 9 8 7 6 5 4 3 2 1

Library of Congress Cataloging-in-Publication Data is available on file.

Cover design by Tom Lau
Cover photo credit: Ken Kreisler

Print ISBN: 978-1-944824-14-3
Ebook ISBN: 978-1-944824-15-0

Printed in China

Acknowledgments

I would like to thank all those who have been with me on this watery journey throughout the years. With way too many relationships in my wake, I can only reach out to everyone who has ever grabbed a line and helped me tie up. To all those at *Power & Motoryacht*, *Yachting*, *Southern Boating*, and *Marlin* magazines; to all my marine industry friends, from fellow scribes to photographers to reps, techs, mechs, designers, builders, advertisers, marketers, communicators, editors and publishers; to Mrs. Cheshir, my sixth grade teacher for telling me I had writing skills and to Mr. Stanley Etkin, my high school English teacher, and Professor Eastmond, my college literature mentor, for inspiring me to write; to all the Jersey Boys & Girls from Long Branch, Oakhurst, and Wayside, the most wonderfully, supportive friends anyone could ever hope to have, you know who you are and more importantly, who I am; to my New York City boat crew, you guys are the best; to Alex Merrill and Tom McCarthy, thanks for the opportunity; and finally to Linda and Sami: mere words would spoil the gift.

Contents

Introduction

"Here today, up and off to somewhere else tomorrow! Travel, change, interest, excitement! The whole world before you, and a horizon that's always changing!"
—Kenneth Grahame, Author

So, you've heard the Sirens' song: irresistible, tantalizing, filling your head with visions of being wrapped in warm, gentle, and comforting winds as you travel across calm azure seas, experiencing sunrises to take your breath away and relaxing during serene moments at quiet coves; encountering adventure beyond your wildest dreams as you travel to far horizons, all to satisfy a void in your life that is now being occupied by terminal wanderlust.

In other words, you want to buy a boat.

Take heed, dear shipmates, for you are not alone. There are many of us fellow sufferers out here—actually, according to the latest National Marine Manufacturers Association numbers, nearly 88 million people in the U.S. participate in some way, with perhaps upwards of 30 million more in such countries as Canada, France, the UK, and Sweden just to name a few others for example—all waiting for you to let go of your terrestrial ties and join us in the pursuit of the nautical lifestyle. And hopefully, this book will help.

I've tried to keep the format simple and easy. Starting with a discussion of boat construction including the techniques used by various builders and what you should be looking for, we'll have a wide-ranging survey of the entry-level boats by some of the major manufacturers including a separate chapter on both the operation and upkeep of inboard and outboard engines, together with the technological advances in control design, after which will follow a thorough discussion on proper boat care and maintenance.

Another important chapter covers the greening of the industry and includes discussions and overviews on how manufacturers and builders are "cleaning up" their processes and what advances are being made in materials and alternative energy sources, including electric and diesel/electric propulsion, solar power, and other cutting-edge technologies.

We'll discuss boat handling, especially around the docks and in close quarters situations including all the exciting and innovative developments in joystick use and the latest pod designs. Seamanship, anchoring, weather, wind, tides and currents, and a summary of the latest in electronic equipment will also be presented.

We'll discuss safety equipment and what to do in the case of an emergency while away from the dock. Also included is a look at insurance coverage, boat loans, and financing, as well as those costs that newcomers to the lifestyle often overlook.

Throughout the book there will also be entertaining anecdotal asides from my nautical travels on how and why our fellow watery wanderers first got into boating, sure to be both amusing and enlightening.

For those of you whose economics are not ready for a new boat, I will also be covering the proper way to navigate the brokerage market, what to look for in a survey—as the stories are legion on purchasing a lemon, this is a *caveat emptor* and absolutely mandatory—and how to pick the right surveyor—equally as important—as well as the new trend and popularity in boat clubs.

While no one book can contain all the information to cover all of boating, it is my hope that the resources presented here will be enough to get and keep you on course for a lifetime of safe and enjoyable boating.

And while you may think that taking the helm for the first time might be a bit overwhelming, trust me, with a bit of patience and understanding your confidence level will soar as you become more and more comfortable every time you leave the dock.

We have a lot of ground to cover so let's kick over our engines, let those lines go, pull in our fenders, and head out.

Fair winds shipmates,
Captain Ken Kreisler

▲ Photo Credit: Peter Frederiksen, Viking Yachts

1 Boat Design & Construction

"I feel there is something almost sacred about building a boat . . . It is almost like creating a living being, a boat seems to have a soul and character all her own. . . . It requires more thought to give a boat a good name than it does a child."
— John Guzzwell, World Circumnavigator

efore I even begin to survey the many boats available for entry-level buyers, I would like to concentrate our efforts first on the basics about boat design and construction. After all, this is where it all begins and having this kind of knowledge will enable you to sift through what you want and don't want.

Boat building has come a long way since our ancient seafaring brethren figured out that if they hollowed out a fallen tree or lashed a number of logs together, they could set out on the water and travel, fish, trade, or even navigate oceans.

Thor Heyerdahl proved this last notion in 1947 on the *Kon-Tiki* expedition as he and his fellow explorers covered some five thousand miles across the Pacific Ocean in a hand-built raft from South America to the Tuamotu Islands in French Polynesia— clearly illustrating that early seagoing people could have made the voyage as well.

Certainly you're not in the market for either a hollowed out log or a raft held together by wooden pegs and rope. You would not be reading this book if you were, but if you so happen to have such thoughts, I strongly suggest you alter your nautical plans to a more terrestrial-based undertaking. Let's center our discussion on fiberglass construction.

The boatbuilding material we know as fiberglass has been around for a long time now and came into being quite by accident. I'm going to skip all the physics, chemistry, and ponderous discussions, but if you really must know this kind of information, there are copious volumes to be found with a good search on the Internet. Me? I'd rather be boating, if you catch my drift. So, let's get right into the good stuff.

In 1932, a member of the research staff at Owens-Illinois, soon to become Owens Corning, by the name of Russell Games Slayter (while I do sometimes digress when I pick up the trail of the obscure and rather esoteric, I am going to bypass the derivation and foundation of Mr. Slayter's middle name; for now that is) while working with a run of molten glass, mistakenly misdirected a jet of compressed air at the substance and, voila! Glass fibers were the result.

Four years after this fortuitous *faux pas,* a patent was issued to Owens Corning for its glass wool *fiberglas* material—back then it was spelled with one "s"—and, because of one of its particular characteristics, it was used as an insulator.

Also in 1936, du Pont introduced resin to its fiberglass—now with the additional "s"; funny how that happens—the result of which was, more or less, the genesis of the composite material we are familiar with today.

Of course it did not take long for one Ray Greene, an Owens Corning person with a definite nautical slant, to see the benefits of this new stuff as a boatbuilding material and set out to design and construct one. It was launched in 1937 but because of the then-brittle nature of the product, the project languished.

There were some other attempts at using the substance to fashion airplane wings for the U.S. Air Force and even a passenger boat, supposedly designed and built in Russia. And for a 1946 prototype of a car with a fiberglass body—which by the way, never did enter the production line—tagged the Stout Scarab, and designed by William Bushnell Stout of the motor car company bearing his name out of Detroit, Michigan. But the best use for the as-yet-to-be-perfected material was waiting patiently for its renaissance. And while there may be plausible argument as to the actual launch date or product-use application of the stuff, there is no doubt that in 1953, together with Owens Corning, General Motors introduced the first real production car with a fiberglass body. Even if you're not a car person, many among us did, and most likely still do, hold a special admiration for the Chevrolet Corvette.

But, and as interesting as this aside may be—Stout, by the way, was also chief engineer of the aircraft division at Packard Motors as well as designing the celebrated Ford Tri-Motor airplane—it's back to the water for us.

Design and Construction

All our boats start out with an idea: a thought, an impression, a concept on how best to combine the ability to be with the water in a use-oriented and safe and comfortable way. And depending on how big the vessel is, there can be

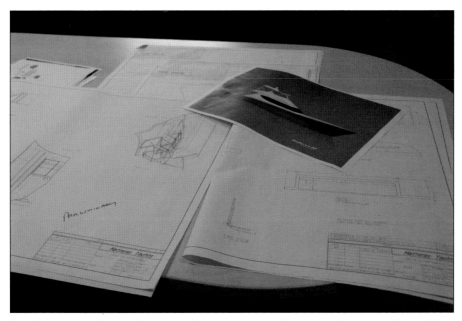

▲ With the vision and talent of a marine architect turned over to fabricators, technicians, installers, and the many others who build boats, someone's dream will become a reality.

quite more than a fair degree of creature comforts able to rival, and sometimes surpass, many opulent land-based dwellings.

But for those of you looking to get into the boating lifestyle for the first time, you are just going to have to lower both your expectations and ability to own "one of those" . . . for now. So, with that in mind, our discussion will center on how your first boat is designed and built.

From all the builders and designers I have spoken with over the years, there is one unifying idea that has run true throughout the conversations: They always use customer input as a major influencing force when conceptualizing their boats. From entry-level bow riders to first cruising boat to major sport fisherman, the input and participation from prospective and repeat owners is highly regarded.

"When we design our boats," began industry friend and design engineer/ marine architect Dave Wilson for prestigious Viking Yachts, "we look at proportions and overall design parameters no matter what size project we are planning. Our owners are pretty specific and we always take that as one of our first considerations."

Kris Carroll, president of Grady-White Boats, had the same take on that subject. "With 15 to 20 percent of our boat buyers being new, first time owners, one of the most important aspects of our entire program is to take care of them and do whatever we can to bring them into the family and deliver the ultimate boating experience."

To that end, and as you start out on your watery lifestyle, one of the most fascinating experiences you can immerse yourselves in is a factory visit. There is not a single boat builder, whether a custom, one-off designer or that of any of the mass production models that does not invite a prospective buyer to their operations facility to see, first hand, the real story on boatbuilding.

"We call, survey, ask questions and do whatever it takes to find out what we need to have happen to make our owners have the best possible understanding as possible," said Carroll. "Getting comfortable with a boat is not the hardest thing to learn. It comes with the territory."

I have been to a wide variety of building facilities covering everything from megayachts to sportfishing and cruising boats to sundecks to PWCs and RIB tenders. I have found each to be quite eye-opening and unbelievably insightful and educational with not only watching the actual construction process, from popping a hull out of its mold to its position on the line, but speaking with designers, engineers, painters, CEOs, company presidents, delivery captains, sales managers, and equipment and systems installers as well.

So that we're all on the same page, and since all of the boat builders you will be considering use these products with this information, here are some

▲ The busy production line at the Grady-White factory. Photo Credit: Grady-White Boats

▲ A brand new, flawless hull is removed from its mold and begins its first voyage down the production line at the Grady-White factory. Photo Credit: Grady-White Boats

of the more frequently used boatbuilding terms including materials, physical characteristics, processes, and descriptions.

Again, let's avoid any discussion on fiberglass or resins that involves advanced physical science concepts and just say that each of the materials used has its own particular profile; its own specific DNA as it were, that makes it suitable for the application.

Lamination: the process of taking several layers of fiberglass cloth and, using an epoxy resin material, bonding, laminating, or unifying them together for strength and support. The strength of fiberglass material depends on the length of its strands, the alternating pattern of how the layers are positioned in the mold, and the temperature and humidity during the process of wetting out, or applying, the styrenated resin. Styrene, by the way, can occur naturally in small amounts in certain plants, but the more familiar use for the clear and colorless liquid derived as a by-product of petroleum is in the manufacture of plastics.

Epoxy Resin: glue-like, semi-liquid adhesive substance that, with the addition of a hardener applied to fiberglass cloth material and left to cure, will become solid. As it holds the fiberglass together chemically and transitions from the liquid to the solid state, resins will allow the material to conform to a specific shape as well as having the ability to transfer the mechanical loads from the fibers to the entire composite part. Epoxies are also very low VOC and can achieve excellent physical properties without post cure.

Wetting Out/Hand Layup: the process of spreading out the epoxy resin with rollers across the surface of fiberglass material and making sure it is fully saturated into the laminate and that there are no air voids before repeating the progression to build up the laminate.

Cure Time: the transition period of an epoxy mixture from a liquid to a solid is called the cure time. It can be divided into three phases: working time—also called open time, pot life, or wet lay-up time (liquid state), initial cure (gel state) and final cure (solid state). The speed of the reaction, the length of these phases, and the total cure time vary relative to the ambient temperature. Epoxy systems do not require high humidity to cure properly. The curing of amine-based epoxies can result in a waxy film called amine blush on the cured epoxy surface. This blush forms when there is humidity and CO_2.

Lamination Schedule: simply put, it is the list of specific materials and orientation of the fiberglass used when building up the layers that make up, for example, the hull or other parts of the boat. Among other things, it includes the weight and style of the weave of the fiberglass material.

▲ Taking care to make sure the resin in fully wet through, the laminate will be built up layer by layer. Photo Credit: Grady-White Boats

▲ Here the fiberglass mat is being cut and fit in the mold. Notice the round ports to accommodate pod engines.

Boat Design & Construction • 7

Tensile Strength: the ability of a material to resist loads or tensions that can pull it apart.

Woven Roving: a heavier, high fiber version of fiberglass cloth, its main use is between the sandwiched layers to increase both the tensile strength, stiffness, and impact resistance of the laminate.

E Glass: the most common type of fiberglass cloth used, so called due to its good electrical insulation properties, it has high strength and stiffness qualities, is resistant to heat and chemical action, and withstands moisture among other traits.

S Glass: fiberglass cloth, known as unidirectional mat, where all the fibers run in the same direction and offers more tensile strength than E Glass.

Prepeg Fabrics: often carbon fiber fabrics that have already been saturated with a resin system and heat-activated curing agent and are ready to be laid up in a mold thus skipping all the other steps in a hand lay-up.

Kevlar: one of the first, high strength synthetic fibers in the Aramid family—those particular lightweight manmade fibers that display excellent heat, cutting, and chemical resistance—to gain acceptance in the reinforced plastic industry. It is stronger, lighter, and more impact resistant than traditional fiberglass and can be used by itself or combined with such other boat building material as carbon fiber. With its high tensile strength-to-weight ratio, it presents itself as five times stronger than steel yet is a much lighter material. DuPont owns the registered name of Kevlar. Kevlar is extremely strong and flexible. Other Aramid materials include Nomex, which is heat/flame resistant, Technora, which is chemical resistant, and Twaron, which is both heat and chemical resistant.

Carbon Fiber: strands of carbon-based materials are woven into a fabric and, using epoxy resin, offer a strong, lightweight, high temperature tolerance with low thermal expansion boat building material that also has excellent chemical resistance. Its high price makes it a bit selective in certain applications.

Chopped Strand: typically blown onto the mold surface with styrenated resin, this random fiber reinforcement material is used as a backup for gel coat to minimize print through and miniscule air bubbles. When wetted out, it conforms well to odd-shaped objects.

Continuous Strand Mat: contains a binder that holds the strand together. During lay-up, it requires styrene to break down the binders to allow for complete resin saturation of the mat. Epoxy does not contain styrene and therefore cannot be effectively used with continuous strand mat. Used when a rapid buildup of a laminate is necessary. This material conforms easily and, due to a binder already present, wets out easily. However, since it is only compatible with polyester or vinyl ester resins, proper bonding with epoxy will not take place.

Biaxial Mat: an ideal material that can be used for repairs, tabbing—used to strengthen, support, and back up the bulkheads and supports within your boat's structure—and reinforcement, the cloth comes in two layers of mat oriented in a 45° fiber angle and stitched together with polyester yarn.

Infusion: often referred to as closed-molded resin infusion or vacuum infusion, it is the technique most considered to be the latest in superior boat construction. Unlike the traditional method of lamination, where the layers of fiberglass material are laid in the mold and hand wet out with a catalyzing resin, using rollers to saturate the cloth and squeeze out any air that might be present, vacuum bagging places the hull or parts, with the dry lamination schedule already in place in the mold, inside a specially designed bag. Once everything is in place the bag is sealed and the air is withdrawn. As this is happening, strategically placed tubes begin to deliver the resin in a controlled manner. The result is a stronger, lighter end product with precise resin-to-cloth ratios, low void content, and a drastic elimination of VOC (volatile organic compounds) into the atmosphere as that given off with an open molded build.

Mold: the actual shape of your boat's hull or part that is specifically designed and engineered along exacting mathematical and physical requirements for the way the boat is going to be powered, used, and the equipment it may be outfitted with.

Most production boat builders will use a female mold with a concave shape; that is, the construction is done from the inside out with the outermost layer going on first with subsequent buildup of the laminate schedule. (A male mold's convex shape laminate build up is done from the outside in, with the outermost layer going on last.) The mold is prepared with a release agent so that when the hull or part is ready, it can literally be popped right out. In addition, that first layer is usually the gelcoat, the thin coat of pigmented resin that allows the finished product to emerge fully coated.

Because you have most likely begun the process and done some legwork, and if nothing else, gazed at stacks of boating magazines, turned the pages of many brochures, and perused the Internet and related websites, you have already discovered there are many types of boats to choose from.

▲ The inside of the mold must be clean and free of any debris, dirt, or imperfections for the hull to come out as perfectly formed as possible. Photo Credit: Grady-White Boats

With your unique position as someone just getting into the lifestyle, the plan is to limit your decision by the kind of boating you wish to do at this point in your nautical career. And that means getting an understanding of basic boat design.

Types of Hulls

For our purposes, there are three types of boats: planing, semi-displacement, and full displacement. And most likely, you are going to be interested in the first.

Planing hull boats are designed to go fast. That's not to say, for our discussion here, that you are going to strap yourself into a high-tech suspension seat, hit the throttles and, watching your fuel gauges drain by the minute, go really fast. But for boats designed and built just for that—you've seen them; those graphic-heavy power and racing boats—fast is a relative term.

A powerboat moving through the water at, let's say, twenty miles per hour, is faster than one traveling at fifteen. But, as we all know, twenty miles per hour is not all that fast. Planing boats are basically designed to get up and out of the water so that there is less drag on the running bottom.

▲ Planing hulls are designed to get up on top of the water.

Semi-displacement boats find themselves somewhere in the middle, having the kind of design that allows them to move through the water a bit more efficiently than the full displacement hull.

▲ Fine classic lines typify the Ellis 28, a semi-displacement design that offers an economical power profile while providing outstanding sea-keeping characteristics. Photo Credit: Ellis Boat Company

Full displacement hulls are typically found on slower boats such as some trawler designs. Generally designed to cruise between seven and nine knots, these vessels are very efficient with power needs and are good in following seas. With a deep and wide hull design, full displacement boats usually have extra room for fuel, more than ample storage spaces, large living areas, and roomy engine spaces.

▲ Well-built, full displacement boats and yachts, like this Nordhavn 40, present yet another side of boating and one filled with the prospects of adventurous long distance travel. Nordhavns have the well-deserved reputation of being able to cross oceans. Photo Credit: Nordhavn

2. The Economics of Vessel Ownership & Picking the Right Boat

"A lot of people ask me if I were shipwrecked, and could only have one book, what would it be? I always say How to Build a Boat.*"*

— Steven Wright, Humorist

I remember the conversation as if it were just yesterday.

"What do you think? Should we buy a boat?"

It was years past now and one late October day when I was on my way south, via Delta Airlines from NYC's LaGuardia to the Ft. Lauderdale/Hollywood Airport, on the annual migration of my marine industry cohorts to attend the first of the twin titans on the seasonal U.S. boat show circuit.

Known to us insiders as FLIBS, the Ft. Lauderdale International Boat Show and MIBS, the Miami International Boat Show, take place within about two and a half months of one another, the former having its epicenter at the Bahia Mar Marina and Resort sometime around the end of October, with the latter one staging across several Miami venues in mid-February. (As of this writing, the Convention Center, one of the main venue sites for MIBS, was undergoing a renovation, and after several contentious court battles, the Virginia Key site had become the 2016 show's new home and for some years to come with the not-associated Collins Avenue Yacht & Brokerage Show, now called Yachts Miami Beach, continuing in the same location.)

The question was lobbed over the aisle to me by a couple with whom I was sharing the fourth row in the front on the plane. I had the aisle seat while they occupied the two cushy leather ones to my right.

Back then, and I am sure things have not changed, company policy forbade us lowly journalists from flying anything other than coach fare but I had accumulated so many frequent miles that I qualified for a complimentary upgrade.

When my name appeared on the tote board at the gate terminal, I happily marched myself up to the podium to claim my prize. And as I recall, the sliced chicken breast over a crispy Caesar salad wasn't half bad at all.

They had seen the familiar magazine logo on my shirt and in the ensuing conversation—which lasted most of the flight and several more times as we serendipitously crossed wakes on the docks—I'm sure I thanked them quite a few times for the strawberry daiquiri and several cinnamon *churros* they insisted I have with them at one of the many floating bars at the venue. But in the event it was only three times, I will now offer a fourth: thank you both, yet again—when I told them my name and passed them each a business card. They were most complimentary in saying as how much they enjoyed the magazine and my writing and video work.

"So, let's boil it down to a simple mathematical formula," I said, smiling and turning in my seat so I was now facing them. "And, please, do not be put off by this. It is just the reality of going into and taking on the financial responsibilities of boat ownership that I think you need to consider. Take the sticker price number you imagine the boat is going to cost you; remember to take into account the electronics and options you may want. Add to that your insurance coverage, dockage, estimated fuel costs, maintenance, seasonal storage if necessary, supplies, and a conservative list of other costs. Once you arrive at that amount, divide it by the total days you *think* you may use the boat, and ask yourself if you have the answer to your question."

Again, do not be put off by this per-use analogy. If you start down that path, you might as well just cancel your golf club membership, eliminate those family vacations, forget about that second lake or oceanside house, or any of the other free-time activities you may want to be involved in, and instead come home after work, or on your weekends and holidays, and watch television and eat potato chips to take up all your spare time.

While you are investing in a product and all its extras that do require a good hard look at your economics, and should those finances make sense to you, what you are buying into is a wonderful and great lifestyle where the money matters associated do not, in any way, mean that the financial side of boat ownership should not be undertaken.

Believe me, it is worth every penny, nickel, dime, and the many, many quarters spent. The memories, the lifestyle, the travel, the camaraderie, the sunsets and sunrises, the experience, the food, the adventure, the friends, all are priceless. For all the many years I have been involved in my watery life, I wouldn't trade them, not a single one, even for having all my credit cards paid off by now.

I bring this up early in the book only because in all my time in the marine industry, and with my ear very close to the manifold as they say, I have seen many a would-be nautical dreamer watch their wish of participating in boating quickly fade away because they did not approach the undertaking with eyes wide open and a very realistic look at the costs. Hey, to be right up front with this thought, if you have the bucks and taking on this added expense is not a problem, I say go for it.

For the rest of you, let's begin by going through the basics. The plan is to help you create a worksheet of sorts to assist in making the right decision. Seeing actual numbers in black and white can often make it easier for you to make the right decisions to take, and stay on, the right course.

To add to this notion, and in a later chapter, I have a segment dedicated to navigating the brokerage market. And it just might be the kind of information you need to perhaps find a perfectly suitable boat, equipped for your needs, that will help to cut down on initial expenses.

Going into this with a budget number in mind, in other words just how much you are willing to commit to as an entry-level boater, the first question we need to address is just what kind of boat are you looking for? What type of vessel will fulfill your needs? Is this a family venture—and if so, please include them in all the discussions, plans, and visits to dealerships or boat shows during the process; trust me here, this is important—or your own personal undertaking? Fishing, day or weekend cruising, perhaps a bit of both? Conceivably going out for an extended voyage now and then?

A daunting undertaking, you're thinking? Take heart, there is a boat for you out there and what I'm going to do is give you a personal tour of the choices that you have and why the boat that you want may not be the one you need.

The first thing you might want to do is get a hold of the schedule for upcoming boat shows in your area. A great resource here in the States is the National Marine Manufacturers Association (NMMA) Website where you will find boatshows.com, a thorough and extensive listing of upcoming seasonal events throughout the nation. If you are interested in looking abroad and will, or have the means to be traveling some time during the year, check out the offerings at boatshowsonline.com as well.

These expositions, whether on the local level or during international gatherings, are ideal places to see everything on the market that may be of interest to you.

Obviously, the purpose of a boat show is to get as many people looking to buy in one place with many a dealer advertising "BOAT SHOW SPECIAL!" And if you are ready, there are actual opportunities to be had as long as you are armed with the right information and knowledge.

▲ When looking for a boat at a boat show, seek out what you are looking for first and then go stroll the docks and dream on.

In the end, you just might be able to score an exceptional transaction, tailor made to satisfy both your budget and your now insatiable and driven need to be a boat owner. I know exactly how you feel.

▲ Keep good notes on everything you see and take lots of pictures. It might be just the right one.

My advice when walking the docks is to arrive early and go right to the displays that are of particular interest to you. In this way, you will be able to gather the information you need without having to wait to speak with someone. Things get really busy during these shows and quality "dock time talk," as the day progresses, does get a bit dicey. In addition, and if you can, opening day, often a Thursday, is preferable if you want to avoid the weekend crowds, "tire kickers," strollers, and dreamers.

If you've been looking at something that has caught your eye, and more importantly your budget, call up a local dealer, visit the showroom, get the basic information—price, add-ons, power options and the like, perhaps go for a boat ride—make sure to leave your check book and credit cards at home—and then make an appointment to follow up at the upcoming show. Trust me, they will be there.

Take pictures—come on, everyone in the world has some kind of a phone that takes pictures— and even some video footage and keep detailed notes of all your conversations, especially costs, financing, options packages, and any other significant matters pertaining to the boat you are interested in.

Make sure you schedule another sea trial; let them take you out for a ride, this time with, hopefully, a fully equipped model—many of the boat shows offer in-water venues where going for a ride is mandatory, standard operating procedure—and show you how all of today's advanced features operate.

As well, this is a great opportunity to get the family aboard and even let the kids and the wife have a go at the wheel. It's easier than you think. Just remember how you felt the first time you sat in the driver's seat of a car.

Do not be cowed, overwhelmed, awed, or intimidated with the operator's prowess. Remember, they have had years of experience. While this may be your first time at the helm, and no matter how uncomfortable you may feel, you too will get there. It's a process and the learning curve is an exciting one. And please, as far as that "BOAT SHOW SPECIAL" is concerned, do not feel the pressure to make the deal right then and there on the dock.

With a reputable dealer, who will most likely honor any conversation already had, there's plenty of time for that after the show closes. But if you are really hot to buy, wait a few days, perhaps even late on closing day, and take a last stroll and drop by to "say hello," if you catch my drift here.

Size Does Matter

Once you have settled things in your mind that you are going to do this, and for a little tactile experience in getting your feet wet before you get out the checkbook, you may try seeking out a friend who has a boat, or a friend of a friend, even twice removed if necessary, who has a boat, and get yourself invited out. And please, do not forget to bring the assorted foodstuffs and other accoutrements for your day on the water and even offer to kick in for the fuel. As most boaters I know are fairly gracious about having guests aboard, you'll most likely get a pass on the latter but the odds will be in your favor to get on the short list when it's time to be invited out again.

Since this will be your first boat, do not have big eyes. I know it is tempting when looking at a 17-foot bow rider to keep glancing over at its 23-foot, twin-engine big sister right next to it and then a quick peek over to that 30-foot, fully rigged, triple engine, center console machine just down the dock. Time to slow down and regroup.

"What we like to tell potential customers, and especially those coming into the lifestyle at an entry level," says Joey Weller, VP of sales at Grady-White Boats, "is to consider, should the personal economics make sense, going up one model size from what you think you may be comfortable with. In that way, once you get into your boat and at ease with handling and its systems—and you will very quickly—you will not regret having something just a little bigger." I see it like this: the smart move just might be to buy your second boat for the first time.

So, just what is an entry-level boat? In this humble marine scribe's opinion, it is one that is manageable in size, power, equipment, and with a price that is affordable for a prospective owner who is, for the most part, unfamiliar with being out on the water on a boat. It is definitely not a car, shipmates, and you can't just drive it away.

In other words, you are a newbie and you are most likely going to freeze, your hands welded to the wheel, knees buckling, and sweat soaking your shirt

▲ With most builder displays at boat shows, a full model lineup will be available for you to look at and compare.

the moment you try and pull away from the dock with your mind screaming, "Why did I do this?"

Have faith. You are in good company. We've all been there in some shape or form during our early apprenticeships. Anyone who tells you different is spinning you a fish tale or has never been at the helm before.

Truth be told, I went from owning a 22- to a 42- to a 93-footer and each and every instance I took the wheel for the first time, I had a terminal case of the heebie-jeebies on top of a major episode of the willies.

To set your minds at ease, today's technology, especially with the latest joystick controls, goes a long way in cutting down on the pucker factor as your individual anxiety level heads north and off the charts. In addition, I don't know of a major boat manufacturer or dealership that does not provide both comprehensive and expert training, instruction, and lessons on all aspects of your boat's operation including practical, hands-on handling and especially docking.

By the time you're done with this tutorial period, you'll have established enough confidence to get you going. And if you still need more time, you can most likely contract your dealer or plug into the vast network of competent boat handlers and captains in your area to give you the added lessons. I'll have more information for you on that a bit later as well. And a final note on this topic: in my experience, there isn't a dock mate, neighboring boat owner, or any marina personnel who will not jump at the opportunity to help out. It's that great of a community.

The Boats

For entry-level opportunities, let's take a look at the lineups from a cross section of manufacturers, listed here in alphabetical order, whose models include many boats that may be of interest to your individual situation.

While this is by no means a complete listing, it will give you some indication of what is out there for you to look at for your first boat.

While each manufacturer will be offering many options, including power and electronics among others, should several of these be up on your radar screen, and when you make your initial inquiry, be sure to ask what the difference is going to be between the base price and that of any additional costs due to an options package. And as pricing may be subject to change, none will be listed here.

ALBEMARLE 25 EXPRESS

Specifications: LOA: 29'10", Beam: 8'6", Draft: 22", Draft w/engines down: 30", Displacement: 7,500 lbs. Easy to handle with enough space for a weekend jaunt away from the dock, the Albemarle 25 can be an exciting getaway boat for first timers. For other Albermarle models, visit the company website at www.albermarleboats.com

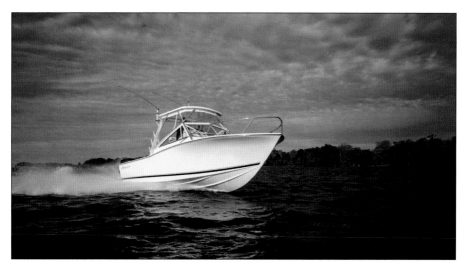

▲ The smart-looking Albemarle 25 delivers the kind of excitement that will welcome you to the boating lifestyle. Photo Credit: Albemarle Boats

ALBURY BROTHERS 20

Specifications: LOA: 20'5", Beam: 7'3", Weight: 2,300 lbs. One up in size from the smallest Albury, the 20-footer is quite manageable both in length

▲ Basic Boating 101 is supplied by the Albury 20. Easy to handle, quick and responsive, she is a great way to day boat. Photo Credit: Albury Brothers

and being operator friendly. Other entry-level boats include 18.5-, 23-, and 27-foot models. For a complete listing visit the company website at www.alburybrothers.com

BACK COVE 30

▲ The Back Cove 30 offers one of the smallest fully equipped cruising boats in the market. Sure to be a head-turner wherever she visits, you and the family will spend memorable time while aboard and traveling. Photo Credit: Back Cove Yachts

Specifications: LOA: 30' 6", Beam: 11' 2", Draft: 2'6", Weight: 12,000 lbs. With a design right from the rugged Maine-built lobster boats, Back Cove's 30 is an impressive family boat that is quite capable of supplying extended weekend trips and longer times away from the dock. Definitely on the higher end of the economic spectrum, and if you have the means, this is a wonderful way to get into boating. For complete information, please visit the company website at www.backcoveyachts.com

THE BAYLINER RUNABOUT SERIES

Specifications: LOA: 22'4", Beam: 8'0", Weight: 3,797 lbs. The Bowrider VR6 is just one of many Bayliners suited for beginning boaters. To view the rest of them, including all the other offerings in the entry-level lineup, please visit www.bayliner.com

▲ Fun on the water is high on the list of the VR6 Bowrider. Bayliner features eight other Bowrider models in the lineup: 160, 170, 175, 180, 185, 190, and VR5. Photo Credit: Bayliner

BOSTON WHALER

▲ A definite mainstay in the industry, Boston Whaler's famed design and stellar reputation offers something for the veteran as well as the entry-level boater. Here, you can begin your nautical experience with the exciting 170 Super Sport. Photo Credit: Boston Whaler

Each of the five different model lines from Boston Whaler offers entry-level boats. And each, like the five models in the Super Sport lineup—the 110 Sport, 110 Tender, 130 Super Sport, 150 Super Sport, and, featured here, the 170 Super Sport—have suitable offerings for the first time boater.

Specifications: LOA: 17'0", Beam: 6'10", Draft: 9", Weight: 1,150 lbs. (no engine). For a complete listing of all models in the long list of Boston Whaler's lineup, please visit the company website at www.bostonwhaler.com

▶ Easy to handle and trailer, the Vortex 203VR is an exciting entry-level boat. Photo Credit: Chaparral Boats

CHAPARRAL BOATS: VORTEX

Specifications: LOA: 20'3", Beam: 8'0", Draft: 1'1", Weight: 2,500 lbs. Chaparral has many offerings in all its model lineups for entry-level boaters and the sporty Vortex 203 VR is just one of many boats you can choose from. Check out the complete listing including H20, SSI, SSX, Sunesta, Signature, and Suncoast models at the company website at www.chaparralboats.com

CONCEPT BOATS 23 CENTER CONSOLE

▲ Fun on the water is the prime objective of the Concept 23CC

Specifications: LOA: 23'7", Beam: 7'5", Draft: 1'4", Weight: 2,100 lbs. (no engine). Another company whose boats are geared up for all sorts of water sports, the Concept 23 Center Console can provide great family boating. For a complete listing of all Concept Boats in the lineup, please visit the company website at www.conceptboats.com

COBALT BOATS

Specifications: LOA: 28'6", Beam: 8'6", Draft: 3'3", Weight: 5,400 lbs. Cobalt offers six different models in its total lineup and all of them have suitable entry-level boats to choose from. The Cobalt A28 offers family fun and excitement. For a complete listing that includes Gateway, BR Series, other A Series boats, WSS, 3 Series, and SD Series models, visit the company website at www. cobaltboats.com

▲ Sporty with racy good looks and performance, the Cobalt A 28 will guarantee great family fun out on the water. Photo Credit: Cobalt Boats

COBIA 220 DUAL CONSOLE

Specifications: LOA: 21'7", Beam: 8'6", Draft: 18", Weight: 2,950 lbs. With a wide range of boats including Center Console, Bay, and Dual Console models, Cobia can deliver the kind of boat that will be able to provide exciting boating for you and your family. To review all Cobia's offerings, visit the company's website at www.cobiaboats.com.

▲ The Cobia 220 has all the bells and whistles for the beginning boater to get started. Photo Credit: Cobia Boats

CUTWATER 24

Specifications: LOA: 23'7", Beam: 8'6", Draft: varies from sterndrive down @ 37" to outboard down @ 30", Weight: 5,300 lbs. for sterndrive model and

▲ Easy to handle and with the added capability of being put on a trailer, the Cutwater 24 makes getting into the boating lifestyle in a very uncomplicated way. Photo Credit: Cutwater Boats

4,900 lbs. for outboard model. There are four other models in the trailerable Cutwater lineup including 26-, 28-, and two 30-foot boats. For a complete viewing, visit the company website at www.cutwaterboats.com

FORMULA 290 FX

Specifications: LOA: 29'0", Beam: 9'0", Draft: 3'4", Weight: 8,950 lbs. Formula has a long list of entry-level models in its Bowrider and Sun Sport lineup, all geared towards getting the entire family involved. Watersports, day boating, cruising and more; it all fits into the plan. For a complete listing, visit the company website at www.formula.boats.com

▲ Family fun from a family run business is what Formula is all about. Photo Credit: Formula Boats

GRADY-WHITE 275 FREEDOM

Specifications: LOA: 26'11", Beam: 8'6", Draft: 1'8", Weight: 4,972 lbs. With a model lineup including Center Console, Coastal Explorer, Dual Console, and Walk Around models, Grady-White has a wide choice of boats for the entry-level, first time boater. Its very popular 275 Freedom has lots of updates and additions. In addition, Grady-White offers its unique Capt. Grady app, a

▲ The Grady-White 275 Freedom will live up to its namesake and a lot more. Photo Credit: Grady-White Boats

confidence-building, breakthrough digital boat systems and operations guide for iPad and iPhone which not only shows you all the features of your new boat but a detailed visual on how to use them as well. It's what you would expect from one of the industry's top builders. For a complete review of all its offerings, visit the company website at www.gradywhite.com

HINCKLEY 29R

Specifications: LOA: 29'2", Beam: 9'1", Draft: 1'9", Weight: 8,200 lbs. The jet-driven 29R and her 29C sistership are considered the entry-level models

▲ An elegant and sophisticated testimony to fine boat building, the Hinckley 29R is often seen on many megayachts as a tender. Photo Credit: Hinckley Yachts

for this prestigious builder and are as expensive as they appear. If your budget allows for a boat like this, you will be more than pleased with your ownership. For more information, visit the company website at www.hinckleyyachts.com

HUNT YACHTS SURFHUNTER 29

Specifications: LOA: 29'6", Beam: 10'6", Draft: 1'6", Weight: 8,000 lbs. Another top-of-the-line builder with a heritage steeped in the legacy of famed naval architect C. Raymond Hunt, Hunt Yachts has several suitable entry-level boats in its Coastal Series lineup including entries in the Harrier, Center Console, and Surfhunter models. These boats are for the prospective owner whose budget affords a bit more ceiling. For more information, visit the company website at www.huntyachts.com

▲ Well designed for comfort and performance, the Hunt 29 Surfhunter offers prestige and good looks.
Photo Credit: Hunt Yachts

JUPITER 26FS

Specifications: LOA: 26'5", Beam: 8'8", Draft: 1'8", Weight: 5,400 lbs. Jupiter seems to have a boat for every need and the 26 FS Center Console is the company's entry-level offering. For a complete look at all the boats from Jupiter, visit the company website at www.jupitermarine.com

▲ Family outings, fishing, fun out on the water; the Jupiter 26FS is all that and more. Photo Credit: Jupiter Boats

MJM 29Z DOWNEAST

Specifications: LOA: 29'0", Beam: 10'2", Draft: 2'6", Weight: 7,600 lbs. MJM occupies a special place in the hierarchy of boat building. The company's visionary leader, Bob Johnstone, was the guiding force behind the establishment of the famed J Boat sailboat design who, together with esteemed marine architect Doug Zurn and Boston Boatworks, have made MJM synonymous with well-designed, well-built, beautiful boats that can take on bad weather if necessary. The 29Z comes in Express, Downeast, and Outboard models. For complete details on MJM, visit the company website at www.mjmyachts.com

▲ The MJM 29 offers strong classic lines, a proven, sea-worthy design, and enough interior space for realizing your traveling plans. Photo Credit: MJM Yachts

MONTEREY 275 SY CRUISER

Specifications: LOA: 27'6", Beam: 8' 6", Draft: 3'6", Weight: 7,200 lbs. Monterey has six models in their fleet with appropriate entry-level offerings in each. For a complete look at the Cruiser, Super Sports, M Series, Surf, Blackfin, and Sport lineup, visit the company website at www.montereyboats.com

▲ Ample cockpit, helm, and forward cabin spaces make the Monterey 275 a great weekend cruiser. Photo Credit: Monterey Boats

RANGER R-25SC

▲ A real stand out wherever they are seen, Ranger tugs offer something a bit different. Photo Credit: Ranger Boats

Specifications: LOA: 27'7", Beam: 8' 6", Draft: 26", Weight, Dry: 6,250 lbs. Ranger Tugs are head turners wherever they are seen and can provide the kind of space you may be looking for in an entry-level boat. Besides the 25SC, the other models include 21-, 23-, 27-, and 29-footers. For complete information, visit the company website at www.rangertugs.com

REGAL 28 EXPRESS CRUISER

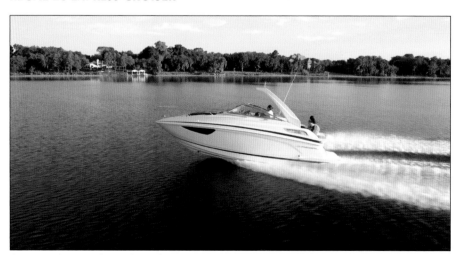

▲ Smart styling with plenty of room for that overnight cruise, the Regal 28 can fulfill your needs. Photo Credit: Regal Boats

Specifications: LOA: 28'10", Beam: 8'6", Draft: 1'10", Weight: 7,585 lbs. Regal has a complete lineup of suitable entry-level boats that will suit any budget and need. From Bowrider to Cuddy to Deck Boat, Express Cruiser and Sport Coupe, check out all the offerings at the company Website at www.regalboats.com

REGULATOR 23

Specifications: LOA: 23'5", Beam: 8'6", Draft: 2'10", Weight: 6,200 lbs. Regulator Marine is noted for its tough builds and throughout the model line-up, no matter what size boat, this no-nonsense approach is evident. Entry-level boats include the 23-footer pictured above, a 25, and a 28 as well. Of course if you think you are ready for this type of boat and experience, you might want to have a look at the 34. To view the complete lineup, visit the company website at www.regulatormarine.com

▲ Fishing fun as well as family day boat activities are courtesy of the Regulator 23. Photo Credit: Regulator Boats

ROBALO 265

Specifications: LOA: 26'1", Beam: 9'2", Draft: 2'8", Weight: 6,340 lbs. With fifteen boats spread out over four models including Center Console, Bay Boats, Dual Consoles, and Walkarounds, Robalo has the kind of extensive profile that makes it ideal for beginning boaters. For a complete look at all its offerings, visit the company website at www.robalo.com

▲ A sporty performer, the Robalo 265 gets you right into the action. Photo Credit: Robalo Boats

SEA RAY 260 SUNDANCER

Specifications: LOA: 26'7", Beam: 8'6", Draft: 24", Weight: 6,667 lbs. Undoubtedly the world's largest production boat builder by volume, Sea Ray's

▲ Known for its excellent use of interior space, the Sundancer lineup offers plenty of comfortable room for family travel. Photo Credit: Sea Ray Boats

lineup includes this entry-level 260 Sundancer, a boat that enables her owners to maximize their time away from the dock. To view the entire model range, please visit the company's website at www.searay.com

SEA VEE 290 CENTER CONSOLE

▲ Fast, responsive, and with fishing DNA, the Sea Vee 290CC is poised for action.

Specifications: LOA: 29'6", Beam: 9'0", Draft: 20", Weight: 6,400 lbs. If you are the kind of prospective boat owner whose vision lies in exciting fishing adventures, the Sea Vee 290 just might be the ticket into this part of your boating life. For a complete listing of all Sea Vee boats, visit the company website at www.seaveeboats.com

Let's Get Started

Once you have your boat picked out, and bargained, compromised, negotiated, and finally settled the deal, gotten all the options you need, and are ready to start your watery career, there is a lot to look forward to. One of the most popular experiences for beginning boaters is to partake in some of the many events sponsored by either your dealership or the boat manufacturer. These include rendezvous, group cruises, marina visits and various get-togethers, dinners, and other like happenings. These are not only enjoyable social events but present opportunities for you to experience what others have learned as well. As a journalist, I have attended many of these sponsored trips over the years and have always had a great time, met very interesting people, and gotten to travel to places far and wide. Make sure you check it out.

What's In a Name?

For this next part of the discussion I am going to take on something from William Shakespeare: *"What's in a name? That which we call a rose, by any other name would smell as sweet."* Of course the quote is from that mother of all tearjerkers and the progenitor of all tragic soap operas, *Romeo and Juliet*, and is a reasonable transition into this thought: now that you've picked out your boat and that particular stress is over, what do you call her?

"We loved our little boat," reminisces my dear friends Arthur and Nancy Roth whenever we speak about their time with their adored *Blueberry Muffin*.

"When the kids were little, we would all go away for weekends. But as soon as their legs got too long for the bunks, they insisted on their own rooms at a Four Seasons. Still, the memories are ones we will always remember with fondness," said Nancy.

So named for the boat's dark blue hull and the family dog, and the fact that Arthur had a rather healthy propensity for the tasty fruit of that particular bakery confection, the name of their vessel was as dear and meaningful to them as the craft they owned.

Naming a boat is a big deal. Most likely, the second most stressful event you will experience behind your purchase—where some of my watery brethren would argue, even before you pull her out of the dock and back in for the first time—is being faced with the decision to give her a name and a proper one at that.

It's very personal and often reflects who, or sometimes what, the owner is all about. *Now & Zen* (a definite New Ager), *Four I's* (most likely an eye doctor

▲ A boat's name says a lot about its owners. But then again, maybe they are balloon enthusiasts.

or the first letter of the last name of a married couple with two kids), *Plan B* (someone whose Plan A obviously worked out), *All Mine* (divorce settlement), *Judy's Dream* (actually the name of a friend's boat whose wife nixed the Harley idea big time and instead let him get the 28-foot center console—it's a long story), *Never Again II, Never Again III,* and *Miss-Take* (all obviously separated at birth)—well, I think you get where this is going. The point is, when you name your boat, choose wisely. It's definitely a reflection on you and as your transom passes other boats, you will be recognized and remembered.

And that brings to mind yet another thought. Why are boats referred to as *she?* Most likely, just as with many esoteric and somewhat impenetrable things we may ponder with some importance, and from all the reading I have done, it seems as if any real thread to the answer may be lost in the folds of time or somewhere in the grammatical assignment of many Romance languages whose word for ship or boat was feminine in gender. However, many salty scholars and nautical linguists point to the more folksy reasons steeped in naming boats after significant and often remarkable women who, in some important way, have impacted the lives of long-gone owners. Case in point? The aforementioned *Judy's Dream.* Lest we push the boundaries here, time to move on.

Boats and Chicken Coops

Eugene V. Connett III was, in every respect, a rare bird. Born in 1891 and passing away in 1969, he spent most of his adult life pursuing the fine art of fly-fishing. And, most likely to support his passion, founded the Derrydale Press, seeking out exceptional and collected works in the sporting field. Whether it was his fishing distraction, or perhaps some bad business decisions, once he ran through the family funds, he found himself bankrupt. However, some insight into his way of thinking, and about his person, can be gotten from this quote: *"Boats are quite different from chicken coops; things on a boat must be able to take any licking to which they are exposed or you take the rap. In a chicken coop the chickens take it."*

Just why this particular thought came to mind, and whether relevant or not, is yet another one of life's great mysteries. I am settled that it occurred and that I could share it with you. All part of the learning curve I suppose. Creativity. Go figure. Anyway, back to the discussion.

Trailering

As all of these boats can be put on trailers, and as you all, because you are reading your very own copy of *Powerboating: Your First Book For Your First*

Boat, I am assuming, most likely, and with a high degree of probability, have never hitched up a boat to the stern of your SUV or similar vehicle capable of performing this function and taken it to your local launch ramp or perhaps, on an overland road trip.

All trailers are not alike. Many new trailerable boats come packaged with trailer and motor, but some don't. So, just what should an entry-level boat owner know in order to get the right one? Features? Extras? Construction? Materials?

"Boat trailers are like any commodity, they range from very good to very poor," said Rick Norman, Sales Manager for EZ Loader Boat Trailers as we discussed a full range of topics related to this equipment.

Jumping right into the conversation, there are some main things to look for when choosing a trailer.

First, if you are a fresh water only user, a wet painted, powdercoated, aluminum or galvanized trailer will be fine. If you boat in saltwater, or fresh and salt, you should limit yourselves to having an aluminum or galvanized trailer only.

In choosing the right trailer for your boat, you need to know the "wet weight" of the boat; that is, the boat, motor, fuel, gear, family dog, and all other equipment that might be aboard, combined. The trailer should carry that amount at a minimum, and having a margin of safety added to the wet weight is preferred.

The trailer should be long enough to have the whole boat on it. A foot or two of boat should not extend rearward past the bunks or roller system. And the transom should be supported.

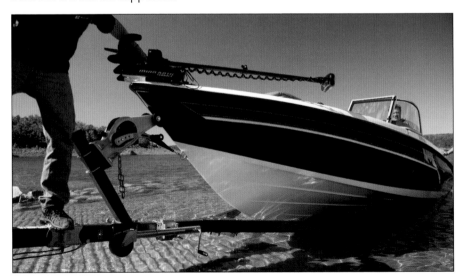

▲ Always pay special attention to all manufacturer's directions to ensure a safe and easy launch and retrieval.
Photo Credit: EZ Loader Boat Trailers

"Always make sure there is ample space between the boat and tow vehicle to make turns without causing any conflict between the two," added Norman.

As far as construction is concerned, there are really only two methods of construction: those that are welded or those bolted together.

According to Norman, welded trailers are strong, and often more eye appealing as they lack the myriad of fasteners seen on a bolt together trailer. However, since they are welded, they are often not as adjustable and become more "boat specific" when they are made. Bolt together trailers are also strong, and can be adjusted to fit a variety of boats. One marked advantage of a bolt together trailer is in any repairs that may be necessary. You can unbolt one part and insert the new one with no welding required.

I-beam and C-channel trailers have one main disadvantage over tubular products in that the wiring and hydraulic brake lines are exposed instead of being safeguarded inside a tubular frame. C-channel is typically not used on large trailers due to strength restrictions.

Some Features to Consider

On the subject of brakes, make sure your brakes meet the state or provincial requirements. Your boat or trailer dealer should have this information as well as any rules and regulations for out of state travel. And when you are ready to roll, have someone standing by to check that your brake lights are on when you step on the pedal and that your turning signals are operational as well.

Load guides may be required where there are currents or winds adversely affecting your loading and launching. LED lighting is preferred as it is brighter and, therefore, safer. Oil bath hubs rather than grease hubs are preferred due to less maintenance. Swing tongues are extremely popular, but are not offered on very large trailers due to the stress they incur.

Buying from a long established company is also preferred for expertise and availability of parts and service over the life of the trailer. Like anything else, reputation and after service are key issues to consider.

Towing Vehicle and Hitches

As far as your towing vehicle is concerned, and if you don't already have a suitable means of transport, it's always prudent not to exceed the hitch or tow rating of your car. If in doubt, check with both your car and boat dealer for their recommendations.

On second thought here, and even before you think of trailering, make sure you have your proverbial ducks in a row so that you are not standing in your driveway, scratching your head and looking at your brand new boat on its brand new trailer with nowhere to go.

There are several different types of hitches for trailers; the conventional 2″ or 2⁵⁄₁₆″ ball—the 1⅞″ ones have gone the way of the dodo—and pintle hitches. The bulk of average retail consumers will have a ball, and not a pintle hitch. Those towing much larger boats than the ones you will be looking at generally use this equipment. I am told Seal Team Six uses them but you didn't hear it from me.

"Most retail people have several items they pull around; travel trailer, atv's boats, utility trailers, and all will come with conventional ball and coupler, so owning one oddball in the group with a pintle doesn't make much sense," says Norman. Plus they are expensive, and the two put together, that being expensive and not needed, make it a rare item for a normal retail owner. And make sure the ball, coupler or actuator, and tow vehicle will all be adequate to carry the gross vehicle weight (GVW).

Even the ball comes in several capacities. There are equalizer hitches that transfer some of the load to the forward axle, but very few can be used in conjunction with hydraulic surge brakes. If you have to have a weight distribution hitch, make sure you either have (a) electric brakes, or (b) a weight distribution hitch specifically designed to work in conjunction with hydraulic surge brakes. Otherwise you may have reduced braking power, or no brakes at all in the trailer. When towing, especially with a tandem torsion axle trailer, it is important to have the trailer fairly parallel with the ground, so an adjustable hitch may be handy in those cases.

How does one know when their boat is safely and properly on the trailer? Assuming the trailer is already adjusted to fit the boat, she will be properly fit when the transom is flush with the end of the bunk/roller system, the bow is seated into the roller or V block on the winch stand, and the vessel is level left and right.

As far as driving techniques are concerned, that can vary greatly with the combination, for example, between towing vehicle and the boat: my boat is huge and my vehicle is barely enough, or my boat is small and my vehicle is huge. The main point would be to make sure the tow vehicle is sized accordingly with the boat and trailer being towed.

When towing, always stay inside the speed limits, use slow steady breaking, not intermittent hard braking, and slow down for curves. If you don't have electric brakes, it may be necessary to put the vehicle in a lower gear when descending long hills to avoid overheating the brakes on the tow vehicle. And make sure you check tire pressures prior to departure.

There's no better advice on backing up other than, when possible, have someone there as a lookout. If that's not possible, put your vehicle in park, set the parking brake, get out and make sure there are no obstructions prior to backing up. And please, when trailering your boat and underway in your towing vehicle, no texting. It can wait.

Launching and Retrieving

So, how best to safely launch and retrieve your boat from a public launch site? Both operations are almost the same whether on a bunk or a roller trailer. The main difference is that with a bunk trailer, the method is a float-on float-off technology, so you have to get deeper in the water with each launch and retrieve.

Before trying to do it for the first time, you may want to ask for help from someone used to the procedures. Your boat dealer will most likely be able to give you detailed and hands-on instructions. A good idea is to negotiate such an arrangement during the sales experience and get it in writing in your final contract. A local marina may also be a helpful place to find someone who can help you out. Again, and as you get more and more accomplished with your skills, the overall boating community is always ready to lend a hand and you will most likely find the assistance you need. All you have to do is ask.

When launching, prepare your boat at the launch area prior to actually going down the ramp, this is as much a courtesy to others as it is to make sure you are ready to splash. Get any items you are planning to take with you in the boat and properly secured. Check that the drain plug is in place and firmly fixed. Most people prefer to unplug the trailer wiring from the tow vehicle prior to launching, but with newer technology, that isn't always necessary. If you have electric brakes, which give you the ability to brake in reverse, you won't have braking in the trailer at the ramp if you unplug your wires.

The rear tie downs on the boat should be removed when the boat is on the ramp and close to the water. Do not remove the winch strap or bow safety chain yet, as some ramps are steep and the boat could unload on dry land.

With everything ready to go, you can slowly back the boat down the ramp until the stern is touching the water. Stop the vehicle, put it in park and set the parking brake. Remove the winch strap and bow safety chain after which you can submerge the trailer adequately to get the boat to float off. Of course, having a person helping that is holding a bowline is essential so the boat doesn't get away when launched.

In loading your boat back on, many people "power on" the trailer using the motor. This is illegal in many states and, in addition, the backwash from the prop can cause damage to the ramp and undermine the end of the ramp where the concrete ends.

The right way to do this is to bring the boat onto the submerged trailer, typically about half way submerged. Again, put your vehicle in park and set the parking brake. Attach the winch line/strap and bow safety chain to the bow eye and winch the boat onto the trailer. Get back in your car and slowly, bring the boat and trailer up the ramp far enough to attach the stern tie downs after which you can drive into the parking area and finish securing the boat, making sure it is properly seated on the trailer and that the brake and turning signal lights work.

On the subject of brakes, Norman lent his expertise to the conversation with some useful insight and information. Hydraulic brakes are called "surge" brakes mainly because the actuator (brake coupler) has to be able to move forward and aft a little bit, and that motion compresses a small plunger inside, which in turn compresses the brake fluid and activates the brakes. The movement accomplishes almost the same thing as applying pressure to a brake pedal in a car.

Most weight distribution hitches have attachments that go from the tow vehicle to the trailer that restrict that movement. The restriction in the "surge" motion can prevent the brakes from going on, or at best, diminish the braking capability. Sort of like putting a small 2x4 under the brake pedal; if the brake pedal can't move, you don't have brakes.

Norman suggests that if the weight distribution hitch is a must, then research the brands that claim they don't hinder braking in the trailer, or, go to electric drum brakes or electric over hydraulic disc brakes, as neither of those rely on surge type hydraulic actuators.

General Trailer Maintenance

As with your boat, you must always keep your trailer clean. In brackish or salt water areas, wash it down as soon as possible. If you have drum brakes, and if your launching facility has a hose setup, flush them with fresh water while still at the ramp. If this is not possible, flush them out generously when you get home. An easy-to-use flush kit makes this job much easier.

As with your pre-start-up checklist before you go boating, so too you should have one for your trailer. Here are some of the basics:

Check:

- all fasteners for tightness.
- the winch strap and tie downs for excessive wear and replace if necessary.
- all lights and turn signals and repair as necessary.
- hydraulic brake fluid level if you have hydraulic brakes.
- all the tires, including those on your vehicle, for proper inflation.
- excessive or unusual wear on the tires and replace as soon as possible.
- all lug nuts/bolts for tightness.
- the wheels for excessive play after jacking up the empty trailer and look for worn or loose bearings. If any wobble is present, have them replaced.
- all disc or drum brakes for excessive wear, and just like on the tow vehicle, repair or replace as necessary.

Other points:

- Remember to drain any water from the boat via the drain plug and don't forget to put it back in prior to launching.
- If you are a seasonal boater and have the ability, store your trailer and boat indoors during those months when you are not boating.
- If outdoors, protect tires from direct sunlight.
- If the boat is to be left outdoors as well, have it winterized and properly covered or shrink-wrapped.
- Vaseline the trailer's light bulb sockets if they are not LED's.

If you want to see some basic visuals on this topic, merely do an online video search on how to trailer a boat and you will get a long list of helpful offerings for you to watch on YouTube and other video hosting sites.

Before we move on, one of the obvious plus factors to trailering your boat can be found in the savings to be had with all the costs associated by docking at a marina and the added seasonal storage if you live in an area where fall and winter boating is not on your Top Ten list. On the other hand, you will have to keep the boat in your driveway or garage—that is, if you have one—and tow and launch the boat at a free public ramp, or at a local marina for a fee of course, every time you want to use it. I know plenty of boaters who choose to launch their boats themselves and have expressed no problems at all with the setup.

Okay then, it's time to get our hands dirty.

3. Basic Maintenance

"Should you find yourself in a chronically leaking boat, energy devoted to changing vessels is likely to be more productive than energy devoted to patching leaks."

— Warren Buffett, Billionaire Financier

*B*efore we begin our discussion I would like to tell what I hope is an entertaining and enlightening story of my own introduction to proper maintenance—or lack thereof.

I began my nautical life by working part time, during my later years in high school, as a yard snipe at a boat yard in the undisputed crown jewel of all the New York City municipalities, that being Brooklyn.

The Schatz Brothers Marina was located in the southeast corner of the borough's Sheepshead Bay neighborhood and the docks that held the fleet of head boats, where I also found pick-up work as a deckhand and mate, was located along nearby Emmons Avenue.

Of course, that memory now reminds me of a time and event that helped shape the mariner I have become. And once we get to the end of this narrative, you will hopefully understand why I consider proper maintenance aboard any boat a major priority.

While researching a theme for an essay I was working on, I found this unattributed quote on the Internet: *"I believe you should live each day as if it is your last, which is why I don't have any clean laundry, because, come on, who wants to wash clothes on the last day of their life?"*

Indulge me here dear readers, as I flex some wordsmithing chops and try to explain how this fits in with this particular chapter.

In a reflective mood one day on just how I got to travel on this life's watery journey I had a most peculiar thought. No, it was more like an image. Actually it was a complete sensory experience that, while involving all of my brain's environmental attention, had in fact isolated and excited the neural synapses of my olfactory and optical memories. Smell and sight shipmates—a little deep-gray-matter tap on the shoulder that asked, "Hey, remember this buddy?"

Now, allow me some leeway here in laying out the foundation for this essay. I promise you, I will try to make it an entertaining read, which hopefully, will begin to materialize in your own consciousness and perhaps unfold your own similar memories as the words line themselves up and the images appear in the narrative. Peeling the proverbial onion as it were.

Back then, the head boat fishing fleet that ran along the Emmons Avenue waterfront was one of the most prestigious and hardy found anywhere, and where things started for me. Sadly, it has shrunk to a mere shell of its former self these days, replaced by dinner cruise boats.

The once proud lineup of boats, many of them refurbished former World War II U.S. Navy vessels, were tied up three to a pier and stern to bow. Their jaunty and salty mates with sun and wind-burned faces, arms, necks, and the white outlines of their sunglasses clearly visible around their eyes and across the bridges of their noses on their five o'clock stubbled faces, were suitably garbed in rubber boots and either yellow or black rubber bib overalls. A few might have one shoulder strap hanging rakishly loose from one arm, and out on the concrete walk, hawking and urging you aboard for a day's fishing,

But back then, in those formative and halcyon days, it was one of the most exciting things in my life and I looked forward to going down there each Sunday afternoon, first as a young boy with my grandfathers, and then on my own when I got older. (Hang in there, we're getting real close now.)

I remember always trying to be at the docks about three o'clock in the afternoon when the boats came back, their horns blaring, announcing their return with the day's catch, soon to be laid out for sale on the sidewalk in wooden crates packed with ice. They had names like *Dorothy B*, *Grace*, *Brooklyn*, *Rainbow*, *Ranger*, *Wahoo*, *Eagle*, *Sea Wolf*, *Rocket*, *Amberjack*, and many others. And then there was the *Carrie D II* and her skipper Captain Sal Dragonetti.

How I had first come to go fishing on her, and then wound up as an occasional mate, splitting my time aboard with mostly working at the aforementioned nearby Schatz Brothers Marina during one summer off from my junior year in high school, is a fairly messy mélange of memories and foggy recollections.

But I do remember being hawked aboard one early morning back then for a day of drifting for fluke as I strolled the quay front with a friend of mine, our fishing rods seated with Penn 60 reels swinging from one hand, a small duffel held in the other containing extra sweatshirts, hooks, sinkers, a 100-yard spool of 15-pound monofilament line, a couple of bottles of Hires root beer soda—one rolled up in the sweatshirt so as not to break against the other—a package of Hostess chocolate cupcakes—you know, the ones with the white squiggle across the chocolate fudge top—often a pb&j sandwich, and usually a piece or three of some sort of chicken wrapped in tin foil and placed in a brown paper bag along with some candy and a couple of Tootsie Roll pops. Unlike today's disappointing confection, back then there was still a fair amount of Tootsie in the pop. I digress.

"Five bucks apiece, ten for the two of you." We got a wink and a smile from the wind- and salt-weathered mate, and I noticed the odor of fish and something else emanating from him even though he stood a good distance away from us. "Two spots left. Whaddya say, fellas?"

She was an old wood tub, painted some kind of orangey-brown on the trim with what still passed as a white hull and superstructure, given the rust stains and whatever else tinted her exterior. She had her pilothouse way aft and a very long foredeck, where on port and starboard sides most of the fishermen had already staked out their territories.

There was some kind of boom apparatus forward that I assumed worked back when she did whatever it was she did before being put into head boat service only to find out later that it was a steadying sail. Whatever. I'm sure it didn't work by then, either. I had already seen the movie *African Queen* and by the looks of what I had paid my hard-earned five bucks to go fishing on, the *Carrie D II* could have been that vessel's grandmother. But my friend and I couldn't care less. We were going out to sea on a warm early summer's day, to go fishing, and that was all we were thinking about when I heard a voice coming from the open forward windows of the pilothouse.

"Okay, let's get it out of here," it said, raspy, gruff, croaky, thick and husky, a disembodied and bellowing declaration from inside that pilothouse.

Our captain, like Ahab early on in Melville's *Moby Dick*, was unseen so far but yet whose presence, I now sensed, pervaded every bit of the boat. What had I gotten myself into here for five bucks a piece, two for ten?

"Get them lines off . . . an' watch you don't let 'em drop in the water like you did last time, ya knucklehead. Almos' caught a wheel, fer Chrissakes." And then the boat shook, making some kind of rumbling noise as if it were a great beast being rudely awakened from a seasonal sleep and now in a most foul mood and undoubtedly, quite hungry.

Thick black smoke coughed and belched from her exhaust ports as the mate skipped fore and aft, slipping and flipping the lines from the port side and up on the pier, each one of them landing with a soft thwacking sound and heralding the signal of one blast of the boat's horn indicating all lines were off. The craft was quickly enveloped in smoke, what with the wind softly blowing from stern to bow as I now clearly recognized the aforementioned fragrance complementing the mate's fishy odor. Lube oil and diesel fuel. Unmistakably a burned and acrid variety of Eau d'#4 Home Heating.

We started to slip down the pier as three more blasts of the horn were sounded—engines in reverse, but you knew that, right?—and by the time we had cleared the end and our phantom skipper had swung the bow to starboard and picked up the channel markers indicating the preferred narrow passage seaward through the bay, its outer sides dotted with many mooring balls, the breeze, now on our port, carried our smoke and scent landward from whence we came.

As we turned the corner of the bay and headed for the buoys that would take us across the Coney Island flats and out to the fishing grounds on the edge of the Ambrose Channel shipping lanes, I noticed the trail of the now dark-gray smoke we were leaving behind.

Fishing was good that day with every long drift producing a flurry of activity for those with the right touch and feel even though, and more than once, someone managed to get themselves all tangled up resulting in a series of salty epithets delivered in various languages and dialects. Two got seasick, most likely from the pervasive exhaust smell since the sea conditions were barely noticeable, and were most emphatic in consigning verbal wills to their friends, adding several supplemental invectives at various times during their explosive episodes of *mal de mer*.

When it was almost time to head back to the barn, I noticed the door on the port side of the pilothouse opening and out stepped Captain Sal for what I was sure was the first time.

He seemed as wide as he was tall with a red-flushed round face littered with a two-day stubble, a head full of wild hair, and big, meaty hands. I had to look back and forth between him and the pilothouse while trying to judge his girth with that of what I perceived was the interior dimensions of his inner sanctum.

I had a most disturbing thought then: there was no head—a nautical bathroom for those of you likely newbies not in the know as yet—that could have had any chance of even remotely fitting in there.

Armed with that information, it was no wonder I quickly willed not going any further with that notion and instead, put that part of my mind under lock and key but not before I just managed to imagine the fleeting image of a five gallon bucket. Like not wanting to look at a train wreck . . . well, you know the rest.

He hitched up his tan khaki pants, and adjusted the tan khaki web belt that hung way below his ample stomach—the cinch that seemed to help prevent said gut from hanging to his knees—and tried to tuck in the back of his khaki shirt. He then gave a shrug of his shoulders, as if the whole ritual was a big waste of time. On his feet he wore some kind of bone-colored, paint-spotted and oil-stained, and much worn boat shoes. Captain Sal, I gathered, was an earth-toned kind of guy.

"How we doin' there, boys?" he croaked to some of the guys fishing at the rail as he flipped the butt of a cigarette up, out, and into the water, and promptly lit another one. Not waiting for an answer, he waddled aft, totally at ease with the gentle roll of the drifting boat, looking at each fisherman's catch, sometimes nodding and other times not, until finally reaching a point on the other side of the boat just opposite where my friend and I had been fishing all day. And we knew where the head was.

"Hey," I heard him say, after which he gave a quick, wet sounding cough and promptly took a big drag on his cigarette.

I didn't know the mate's name was Hey; I thought it was Dave or something like that. But he answered, "Yeah Cap?" as he made his way forward after netting a fish for someone near the stern.

"Go on down there an' check the earl, will ya. I'll be kicken' 'em over and this'll be the last drift. It's almost time. Hiyadoin there boys?" he said to me as I looked over to where Hey had now joined him.

"Got some nice fish," I said as my friend brought up a very big sea robin, swung it up over the rail, and plopped it down on the deck. The hook came out fairly easily and he stood up and was about to throw it back overboard.

"Don't be trowin' dem big ones like dat back in. I got some Portogeese guys taken 'em," he said. And that came out as *Por-toe-gee-sea*, just to key in on Captain Sal's proficiency at pronunciation. Just saying.

"What?" I think my friend said as the fish wriggled and slipped out of his hands and splashed into the water.

"Fer Crissakes," Captain Sal said as he shook his head toward the deck, the cigarette now dangling from his mouth.

"Ah, what the hell. Go on now, check that earl so's we can wrap this up," he said to Hey and, brushing past him, made his way aft, down the starboard side to the other door that led to the pilothouse and in he went. A moment later, a cigarette butt launched itself out of one of the side windows and I had no doubt, another was promptly lit up.

As Hey emerged from the depths of what I gathered was the engine room, wiping his hands on an oil-stained rag, and looking towards the pilothouse, he gave a thumbs up sign after which came three quick toots of the horn signaling all lines up.

The *Carrie D II*, heretofore under the influence of the somewhat hypnotic and low decibel rumble and vibration of the generator, constantly emitting its own noxious fumes from a hull vent, suddenly reverberated with the sound and shuddering of the main engines, and began to shake itself from stem to stern. First one, then the other started followed by the billowing black smoke.

There was some sort of announcement that came over what passed for an amplified sound system aboard, but with the hanging rusted speaker secured by some piano wire and duct tape to keep it from flopping and banging off the side of the pilothouse from the lamp wire that snaked its way out of a disastrously drilled-out hole there, the words and message were wholly unintelligible.

"Pool fish in the stern," heralded Hey, acting as interpreter for the other-worldly, public address, static-laden communication as he made the rounds of the deck. "I clean the fish too, for fifty cents each." By the time we docked, the trail of dark gray smoke that had been following us around finally dissipated into the late afternoon sky.

I think by now I've painted a pretty clear picture of what kind of boat the *Carrie D II* was and how she was an unfortunate reflection of her skipper. I would imagine that in her heyday, those first few years after her launch, she was a pretty tidy craft. And while my friend and I continued to fish on her—that five bucks apiece/two for ten deal to a pair of soon-to-be high school seniors suited us just fine—and even managed to win a pool or two, I would not realize the full extent of what I had only imagined was below decks until one mid-summer trip.

Just as I was about to get off one day, Captain Sal, leaning out of the lowered window of the pilothouse's port side, and flicking a butt into the water, said: "Hey kid. I notice you're pretty much a regular. I may need an extra deck hand. Wanna make a few bucks an' fish for free?" he said as yet another cigarette appeared and was as quickly lit, a cumulus cloud of smoke momentarily blocking out his face. "Well, whaddya say. Yes or no. This ain't no math test."

"I have another job over at Schatz. In the yard. I'll have to check what days I work each week. It changes," I remember saying, already with the lure of free fishing and a couple of extra bucks in my pocket presenting some tantalizing low hanging fruit to me.

"I know dem guys. Sometimes when I got to get a wheel dinged out, I go there. Out and in the same day. Haven't been since last year though. Okay den, you let me know. But don't wait too long. I got a lot of guys want to work this boat," he croaked, coughed, and took in a long drag.

"Okay," I said and turned and got off the boat and looked back one more time.

"Free fishing an' you get tips an' the boat gives you a few bucks," he said.

I managed to get a schedule that gave me Tuesdays off and since the yard was a short walk from the fishing boat piers, I left a message for Captain Sal that I could give him Tuesdays for the rest of the summer.

Hey—his real name was Brad and for as long as I worked the decks, I never heard Captain Sal refer to him by another handle—and I got along just fine and I had no problem in acknowledging that he was the Alpha mate on board the *Carrie D II*. None whatsoever. But now being the new guy, I was relegated to perform all the slop jobs Hey/Brad was doing before. Like Ishmael, again channeling Melville, I signed my soul over to Captain Sal Dragonetti.

Shape-up was at six a.m., and we usually tried to pull out of the dock by seven. While Captain Sal was out getting bait or whatever, Hey/Brad and I started to square things away for the day's trip as a few of the regulars started to show up and grab their usual spots. I was shown the engine room hatch and, with a dirty old Boy Scout flashlight—you know, the olive-green one with the ninety degree bend to it, this one so oily I could feel the residue on it—stuck in a back pocket of my jeans, descended into the dark inner domain of the *Carrie D II*.

Now, in those days, my entire knowledge of working machines and wiring and pumps and filters and couplings and generators and harnesses and transmissions and expansion tanks and head gaskets and well, just about anything that concerned making this boat move through the water, was as nil as could be, making me as dumb as a bag of hammers when it came to operating anything.

As I made my way down the slippery metal ladder, my hands getting oil-stained as I went from rung to rung, until finally alighting on the engine room deck, still feeling that slippery, sliding effect underfoot, I looked around. The only light was that from the open hatch above and I scanned the densely packed space for a switch or a cord that would illuminate the place.

"Hey," I yelled up at the open hatch above, smiling as I did and then adding, "Brad!" Only a few minutes aboard and I was already taking on Captain Sal's persona. I wondered about how Hey/Brad's mind had so far been affected what with him being, more or less, permanent ship's company.

"Yeah," he said, peering down into the hold.

"There a light switch down here?"

"Port side. Behind the generator. But if it don't work, maybe the bulb is out. Use the flashlight. Dips're on the inboard sides of the engines. Also, check the oil in the generator too. But it's on the outboard side so you'll have to do some climbing over it. Sal'll be back soon and want to fire it up, so let's get going. If you need to add any oil, look under each engine. There's a space there where we keep it. Fill it just past the top mark on the dips."

There was a good reason the light did not come on when I located the switch box. There was no bulb in the overhead socket. Actually, the screw-in neck was there but the bulb was not, and I found a few remnants of broken glass underfoot as I stepped between the main engines. I took the flashlight out of my back pocket.

Suffice it to say, Dr. Frankenstein's lab had nothing on the engine room space aboard the *Carrie D II*. The overwhelming smell of oil and diesel fuel, mixed in with a rather raunchy bilge odor, permeated everywhere and, with the hatch open, most assuredly wafted upwards. I was already enveloped in its bouquet and quickly realized how it followed Hey/Brad wherever he went. Now, I too was so baptized and anointed.

All three engines, the two mains and that of the generator, with their weeping cylinder covers streaking the blocks, needed oil. As I scanned the underneath areas under the now yellowing glare of the Boy Scout flashlight, the only things I could find there were about a half-dozen, oil-stained quart milk containers. I lifted one, feeling the weight of some liquid and, pinching the lid open, looked in.

It was oil all right and even under what I knew was the quickly fading light of the flashlight, I could see it was very black and thick. I found a funnel and fitting it in the oil fill, started to pour the viscous liquid in. It only took a few minutes, even with having to climb over and then straddling the generator, to get it done.

Before climbing up and out of what surely was the inspiration for one of Dante's rings of Hell, most likely the Seventh, I gave each engine a quick coolant inspection as instructed in the recent past by one of the mechanics at the yard. I twisted the cap off, stuck my finger in and if it came up wet, it was okay. Today, all was fine.

Finally getting back to the surface world, after what seemed an eternity, I realized I was now covered with the kind of dirt and filth quite unlike that which I picked up while fishing, with the latter being totally acceptable.

The spaces under my fingernails were black and there was a wide swath of gunk across my gray high school sweatshirt that also covered the waist area of my jeans. There was a black smudge across the top of my right hand and a matching one that ran across my brow. The palms of my hands were dirty and oily and I felt as if I were walking on a film of it as well. And of course, there was the smell.

Captain Sal waddled aboard a short time later. He wheeled a rusted hand truck from his beat-up van piled high with about 24 white rectangular boxes, 12 of each containing a frozen block of squid and spearing. Then he let himself, step by step, down the boarding ladder. It was dead low tide and with no floating docks along the entire waterfront and all the boats rose up and down. By the water trail it left I could see the bait was already beginning to thaw. Captain Sal did not drive a van with a refrigerated compartment.

"They ain't gonna get aboard by themselves," Captain Sal said to me as he tried to hitch his pants up above his ample belly, gave a "thumbs over there" signal, and disappeared into the pilothouse.

Think what you want about the *Carrie D II*, but we always had plenty of bait aboard, what with the leftovers being added exponentially from the day before, albeit some of it, by the time the later part of the week rolled around, was getting a bit ripe and added to the overall multi-fragranced odor that always accompanied the boat.

I heard the low rumble of the generator coming to life, saw the belch of black smoke snaking up over the aft port rail from the exhaust port in the hull there, and recognized the crackle of the VHF radio as he turned it on. With a couple of buckets of salt water drawn from the bay to thaw out the bait, Hey/Brad and I got things ready for the day's fishing.

This was the routine aboard the *Carrie D II* for all the trips I made on her for the rest of that summer. I indeed fished for free, made some tips, and got some bucks from the boat.

For the most part, boats like the *Carrie D II* were already on the other side of the changing times. And as it turned out, even though she was an old tub and way past her prime with many of the other boat owners already bringing in newer, faster, and more comfortable head boats, and Captain Sal was as an irascible character as there ever was, still it was loads of fun as the days slipped by and I went from being a high school junior to entering my senior year.

Nowadays, whenever I have the opportunity to drive along the Belt Parkway, that famed roadway whose construction began in 1934, girdling the edges of waterfront Brooklyn, whether going east or west, I often take the Coney Island exit and stop at Nathan's Famous for a quick hot dog, greasy fries, and a root beer soda, after which I make my way to Emmons Avenue and begin a slow crawl, gazing out to the right at the concrete piers.

It's changed so much to my memory's eye that I find it almost unrecognizable. But still, the sights, sounds, and experiences that set me on my life's course are there for me to bring up once again, whenever I please. And coming full circle in this bit of nostalgia that I have been sharing with you, are the images of Captain Sal Dragonetti and the boat and machinery space aboard the *Carrie D II* and the place it occupies in my consciousness as what could be, maybe the filthiest engine room ever.

Indeed, so vital was that early experience that by the time my apprenticeship really began to take shape and I embarked on securing various nautical positions as I moved along, it became easier and easier to work around all kinds of boats and owners and captains.

I quickly saw the advantages of eventually getting my 100-ton ticket and thus was able to see my way through undergraduate, graduate, and post-graduate college and university studies as a charter boat and yacht captain. Not a bad way to go. And I was always cognizant of keeping whatever vessel was in my charge absolutely clean and smelling real nice.

Anyway, coming full circle, my aforesaid yard snipe apprenticeship saw me basically cleaning up the grounds, scraping and painting bottoms, fetching the left-handed screwdrivers—yeah, I fell for that one—and carrying out most of the grunt work for the workers, some of whom were often hard-drinking, cigarette smoking, foul-mouthed individuals who just happened to be the best at what they did; from woodwork and painting and varnishing, to engine tear-down and repair and electrical wiring, to fabrication and upkeep, to putting a boat into a slip without even looking, they were masters at their particular crafts. And even at that young age, I knew I had fallen into something special and worthwhile that could lead to something going forward.

Keep It Clean: Exterior

Let's start with your boat's finish. As discussed previously, gelcoat is the hard outer coating applied to the fiberglass while it is still in the mold. Put on in its liquid state and left to cure and harden, and besides the high gloss shine it gives once polished, it protects the fiberglass from being degraded by ultraviolet rays from the sun.

However, left to the elements, the glossy shine will be replaced by a dull, chalky appearance—a condition known as oxidation. In this state, gelcoat can lose its protective properties and become somewhat porous. If ignored, it can

▲ Keeping your boat's gelcoat clean and shiny requires proper washing. Doing so will have it always looking bright and in shape to do its job.

lead to the dreaded condition known as hydrolysis. This latter situation occurs when water actually infiltrates beyond the gelcoat and mixes with the resin used in the lay-up process.

The result provides the foundation for situations that can cause blistering. This comes about more often when water gets through the gelcoat due to hairline, spider, stress, or any other kind of crack, and gets cozy with the water-soluble chemicals in the resin. In a short period of time, and as the pressure increases with more water finding its way in, the gelcoat will bulge outwards with the buildup.

In some severe cases, delamination can take place as well. This is where there is actual separation of the fiberglass cloth from the resin or from the core holding them together. While not necessarily the end of the world if caught early enough as far as repairs are concerned—left to fester however, the conditions can become widespread and prove to be disastrous—but to be clear, both are not good and every precaution should be taken to avoid any opportunity for these situations to take root in your boat.

For example, if you have hit or even bumped the dock once too often, or smacked some floating or underwater object, you need to have your marina service manager take a look. Quick action can save you a lot in repair costs when it comes to some straightforward preventive maintenance at the time of the incident.

▲ Using the right brush for the right job will result in the kind of finish that always looks bright and shiny.
Photo Credit: Shurhold

Being careful about your boat-handling skills—do not hesitate to put out an extra fender to two during your early days on the docking learning curve—and doing a thorough and complete wash down with fresh water as well as a good scrubbing with a soft brush and biodegradable liquid soap is your first line of defense.

Soft brushes, either handheld or on the end of a telescoping handle, are the ones to be used on the hull and smooth finishes—as not doing so can cause scratches—while a harder, and more aggressive bristle takes care of non-skid areas and decks. And for you salt water boaters, make sure you keep your glass windshields streak-free and clean of all residues.

The importance of keeping up with your cleaning regimen cannot be overstated. I am sure, if you've been strolling the docks, you have seen many a boat owner at work, polishing, shining, soaping, and looking for any errant fingerprint or blemish that may mar the exterior finish.

It is, as far as I am concerned, a labor of love. No matter what size, shape, or configuration the vessel may be, there are very few things more heartwarming to a boat owner's eye than a well-kept craft, especially the one they own.

I've seen many an owner, newbies included, hire professional cleaning crews to get the job done. And while I am a big fan of free enterprise and entrepreneurship, with a little elbow grease along with the right tools and products, anyone can get showroom new results.

For example, and while there are many fine products on the market for the job, I've had excellent results with many of the offerings and tools from Shurhold (www.shurhold.com).

The company site not only highlights the long list of offerings in its catalog, but also provides helpful guides for various maintenance projects and presents excellent videos as well.

Compounding and waxing, while time consuming and a bit labor intensive is an excellent way to keep your hull looking bright and clean. It's also a good group task that you can get the kids going on or to get some payback from your freeloading friends.

Begin with a thoroughly washed hull and removal of all the loose dirt and grime. Once done, it's time to slap a clean buffing pad on the machine.

With this particular kind of work, it's best to use a random orbit polisher—Shurhold's Dual Action Pro for example—that is light in the hand and easy to use. The technique is not hard to learn or get comfortable with.

According to their guidelines, you can use a clean paintbrush to apply enough of the buffing compound—here, the company's Buff Magic product—to cover a 2' x 2' section with a small "X" pattern.

As with most applications, more is not better. With the way these quality products are produced and formulated, their compounds have the ability to

▲ With the right tools and a little bit of patience, your boat's finish will always be looking good. Photo Credit: Shurhold

break down into finer and finer particles the more they are polished. Therefore, as you continue to work the product in, the more thorough and effective the application will be.

Once you have the area properly covered, it's time to put on your safety glasses—I am a big advocate of eye protection when doing any kind of work that may result in any chance of a foreign object or substance getting into your eyes—and apply the pad to the boat before turning the polisher on at low speed. This will prevent any of the applied material from being sprayed off the surface.

Work in an overlapping, up-and-down pattern, and then side-to-side, at a steady pace. Trust yourself, you'll get the hang of it. Apply gentle pressure to the machine and continue working until the area is completely done. Now you can stop and examine the area.

With a microfiber towel, wipe away the excess compound. Depending on the oxidation, it may take two to four passes with the polisher to bring back the shine. Repeat as needed until the desired level of shine is achieved.

The debate of using regular cotton towels versus microfiber towels on painted surfaces, fiberglass, vinyl, and Plexiglas has been long-standing. According to Shurhold Industries, which is a solid supporter of the microfiber choice, using them will further protect the surface finish from fine scratches.

▲ Microfiber towels are easily cleaned by simply tossing them into the washing machine.
Photo Credit: Shurhold

The softness of microfiber towels comes from their composition of polyester and polyamine, which are thinner than human hair. They absorb 98 percent of water, whereas cotton can only absorb 70 percent at most. Microfiber also picks up dirt, oil, and other contaminants and locks them away in the tiny hooks of the fabric until it's washed or rinsed. Regular cotton just pushes the dirt along the surface, again increasing the chances of scratches and imperfections.

Microfiber towels are elastic, resisting tension and returning to their original state. They are safe to use with most chemicals and are easy to wash either by hand or in the washing machine, as long as fabric softener isn't used.

Continuing with our hull cleaning, when moving to a new 2-foot-square section, overlap the previous section by 6 inches to avoid missing spots. Ensure the pad is clean and free of debris in between areas for maximum effectiveness.

As mentioned, Shurhold has an instructive video detailing this entire process and you can grab a look at it at the company website.

On the subject of any stainless steel trim aboard, it should also be washed with fresh water and soap, dried off and then wiped down with a proper cleaner designed to protect the finish.

▲ Stainless rails require the right kind of attention to keep them in the best condition possible, especially in the saltwater environment.

Should the outer layer be compromised due to accumulated minute build-ups, such as salt deposits during use or even those that collect at the dock, it will be open to pitting and corrosion. There are many fine products on the market that are readily available at your marina store or larger outlets such as West Marine, Home Depot, and Ace Hardware.

In keeping up with any Isinglass, EZ2CY, or Strataglass products—the clear vinyl or polycarbonate material that makes up those familiar plastic enclosures—care must be taken to ensure they are always in tiptop condition. I am sure you have seen some that are faded, scratched, yellowed, or held together by duct tape, which is very tacky and not nautically proper at all. You will be shunned by your fellow mariners should you present your boat in this manner.

As they are easily scratched and can be affected by grit, salt residue, bird droppings and whatever, once they are, it's most likely forever. While light scratches can be removed by using several products on the market, deeper ones present more of a problem.

It's important to remember when cleaning your plastic enclosures to make sure you hose them down with fresh water first, this to remove any accumulated deposits such as salt, dust, or any other debris before wiping clean with a soft chamois or clean cotton cloth. In this way, anything on the surface area that can cause the material to get marked will be eliminated.

Do not use abrasive paper towels, as they can produce what may start out as minute and insignificant scratching and develop into a much more serious condition. Avoid those products containing alcohol such as Windex as they can make the plastic material soft and tacky. I know of excellent results with Meguiar's Mirror Glaze (www.meguiarsonline.com), Mermaid's Plastic Cleaner (www.mermaid.com), and Plexus Products (www.plexusplasticcleaner.com). The all get high marks.

Take some good advice; wash down your plastic enclosures before you go out because residue may have settled on them during the night. If you go to roll them up, you may scratch them in the process. Of course, give them a proper cleaning when closing up for the day. And if you tow your boat, take them down before hitting the road as kicked-up dirt, rocks, and other particles from vehicles ahead of you can cause somewhat more severe damage given the speed at which you may be traveling.

Should you be a seasonal boater, when it's time for winter storage, lay your enclosures flat and on a clean sheet, placing sheets between them as well as on top as a cover. And make sure they are in a place where no one will walk on them.

My recommendation is if you stay on top of your cleaning regimen your boat's finish will always be in top shape.

Zip Tip

If there's one thing that irritates me more than a backed up toilet or losing an engine to a clogged fuel filter it's those annoying plastic zippers or snaps that always seem to get stuck, or are hard to negotiate, on a boat's canvas and plastic enclosure. To help you deal with this situation, which happens quite often especially in the saltwater environment, Shurhold (www. shurhold.com) offers its SNAP-STICK lubrication stick. Another zipper and snap lubricant product that I've seen used successfully is from IOSSO (www. iosso.com). Keeping the zippers and snaps clean with a fresh water wash and a quick rub down with a hand brush and soap, along with a lubricating swipe now and then, will keep them operating smoothly. You can also use a Q-tip cotton swab to easily apply any suitable lube to snaps as well.

Caring for your canvas covers should also be part of your everyday wash down. As most of these items are manufactured and supplied by the Sunbrella Company, it is their recommendation that the woven acrylic fabric, with its mildew, water repellent, and UV resistant finish, first get a good brushing off to remove any dirt or debris. After that you can wash the entire canvas by giving it a thorough fresh water soaking and a soft scrub down using a mild

▲ Keeping your canvas covers clean and dirt free is all part of the overall maintenance regimen for your boat.

non-detergent liquid soap such as Lux or Ivory. Following a thorough rinsing to get all the soap off, let the fabric air dry.

If your boat's canvas has been used as a bombing run for the local bird population—often seeming to be a rather fun sport for our avian brethren, the results of which are splattered and splashed all over—there are several products that can help.

Nixalite of America (www.nixalite.com) offers their Poop-Off, a biodegradable cleaner originally developed for sensitive environmental areas that uses natural enzymes to break down and dissolve the mess. Other suitable cleaning products include those from available from StarBrite (www.starbrite.com), Boat Brite (www.boatbrite.com), Meguiar's APC, Bell Chemical's Roll-Off (www.bellchemical.com), Spray N' Wash, a product that is most likely in your laundry room at home, and Raritan's CU (www.raritan.com) among others.

As bird droppings are quite caustic—especially from those sea birds we all know and love who eat anything and everything from fish to beach leftovers to the five star gourmet meals found at inland garbage dumps and landfills and then digest it; just think of what kinds of gastrointestinal juices it takes to make that happen—it's always best to get them treated as soon as possible.

If you don't have any of these products on hand, wet down the surface with lots of fresh water and pour enough mild non-detergent liquid hand soap on to cover the spot. Wait at least twenty minutes for the soap to soften things up a bit and then gently scrub the stain with a brush. You may have to repeat this several times until the spot is gone.

TOP TIP

If the stain proves somewhat inflexible, try mixing a half cup of non-chlorine bleach with a quarter cup of natural liquid soap (try perusing the products available at www.soap.com) in a gallon bucket of water. Using a soft bristle brush, wash the area and let the mixture sit on the stain for about twenty minutes before rinsing off. If necessary, you can repeat the process. While there are many other grass roots recipes for this, before using any, as well as having any questions about any other fabric cleaning products, make sure you check with Sunbrella first (www.sunbrella.com).

Keep It Clean: Interior

The end game here is to keep your new boat looking and smelling like the day you first took the keys. The big problem you may have to face as far as, that is if you have one, the interior of your boat is concerned—how neat you keep it is your personal dilemma; if you choose to keep it like a frat house, well you own it—is watching for any sign of mold and or mildew. And yes, there is a difference.

While both are fungi growths, mold presents itself as fuzzy in appearance and can be blue, green, yellow, brown, gray, black, or white in color. Mildew's usual growth pattern is flat and can have a powdery or downy appearance. Left to grow, the former begins as white in color and can change to yellow, brown, or black with the latter starting out as yellow and becoming brown. This stuff is the perfect subject for a Stephen King horror novel.

Even as some molds are used to create a number of the world's most delicious cheeses as well as being responsible for the miracle of penicillin, it can also be the cause of many health issues including respiratory problems, allergic reactions, headaches, and other negative ailments. Biological cousin mildew has zero beneficial uses. My advice, eat cheese, stay healthy, and keep your boat clean.

But before you call your boat dealer and cancel your order, there are some simple steps you can take to prevent these annoying interlopers from creeping aboard.

Consider this: as most of us will be doing our boating in nice climes and usually on warm, sunny days, any moisture in the air that does collect aboard, and in particular within enclosed spaces, will condense during the cooler night time hours.

Moisture prevention and keeping things dry is the key and proper ventilation is your first line of defense. And, whether you trailer or not, your boat will be spending most of its time in and around water, and the chance of dampness being present is quite high. On the flip side, if you use your boat on a regular basis, or are a year round boater, and keep up with making sure you do not let water/moisture accumulate, the odds of encouraging this kind of problem aboard is greatly diminished.

With center console models, bow riders, or any other design that do not have enclosed accommodation spaces or a head compartment, the main concern will be with all of the hatch areas where water can collect and be ignored. To avoid this situation, when the day is done, and during your wash down routine, open the hatches, clean the interiors with soap and water, especially in the channels, and, using a chamois cloth, make sure they are completely dry before closing things up.

With boats that do have enclosed spaces, whether a V-berth or those with larger quarters, including perhaps a shower/head compartment, a little extra care should be taken.

Make sure everything is wiped down and dry. If you keep your boat in a marina, and buttoned up each night, you may want to install a small fan to keep the air moving.

But for pontoons, kayaks, canoes, or paddle boards, no matter what model or design of boat you have, you most likely have a bilge area that must be kept clean and dry as well. Being at the lowest part of the hull, it is here where not only water can accumulate, but also for those of you running an inboard engine, oil, antifreeze, and other materials usually collect. The result can be a stinky mélange of some rather foul odors.

What I recommend here is to lay some absorbent pads—available at any marina store—in the bilge areas, fore and aft, and especially under the engine often. Check them on a regular basis and make sure when you bag them up, as more than not you will have some oil residue sopped up as well, you dispose of them in the proper manner and through your marina manager.

Keep It Clean: Bottoms

Now, let's get on to having our bottoms painted.

If you are fortunate enough to have a lift at your home dock, or dry stack your boat at the marina, or trailer and launch/retrieve each and every time you use your boat, you most probably do not have to use protective bottom paint.

For the vast majority of us who either keep our boats in the water for several months, or enjoy a year round season—oh, how I envy this group—getting the proper protective coating on the bottom is essential.

To guard against unwanted organisms, including barnacles, slime, and aquatic growth adhering to the bottom of your boat, it is necessary to coat it with the right kind of paint.

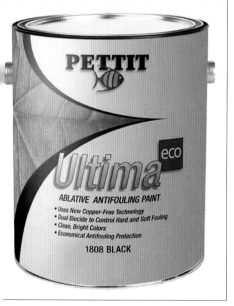

In years past, when we weren't so attuned to environmental issues—and just what was everyone thinking? That whatever we were dumping, burying, aerating, burning, pulverizing, decomposing, evaporating, trying to neutralize, sending to the bottom of our oceans, and any other of a myriad of noxious, toxic polluting practices was not going to haunt us later?

Most of the bottom paints, known as antifouling paint, contained high amounts of tin. Used as a biocide—ready for this definition? A biocide is a poisonous chemical agent, such as many pesticides,

◀ If your boat sits in the water, you are going to need antifouling paint on the bottom. Photo Credit: Pettit Paint

used to destroy life. There's more, but enough said—tin has been banned throughout the world due to its uber toxic qualities as it found its way into the water wherever it was used.

Today's antifouling paints are basically copper-based and the more present, the better protection is afforded. The most popular paints are those with ablative qualities.

That is, they wear down over time much like a bar of soap does as you use it. With such product selections as those from Interlux (www.yachtpaint.com), Pettit (www.pettitpaint.com), and Sea Hawk (www.seahawkpaints.com), you get to choose the kind of protection that is appropriate for your particular use. Each of these fine companies offers excellent guidelines for use including surface preparation, application, care, proper disposal of used materials— very important—and other vital information together with any environmental issues. Given the nature of the product, many state and local laws forbid any do-it-yourself work and instead, it must be done by your local marina service center, especially with any seasonal reapplication. Make sure you check with them first as to the rules for your area. Not doing so may incur some hefty fines.

Marine Toilets

To wrap up this chapter, let's cut to the chase here, shipmates. You DO NOT, under any circumstance, shape, manner, or form, want to, pun obviously intended, mess with your marine toilet. I'll take dealing with sopping up bilge water rather than hear the dreaded news that something is wrong with the boat's MSD . . . the marine sanitation device.

The best way to prevent any problems, no matter how small, is to become familiar with the particular operation of your system, its parts, how they work, what can go wrong and why, and what you can do to head off any confrontations with it.

For most of us, our concern is with a Type III U.S. Coast Guard approved Marine Sanitation Device that is designed to simply hold waste material for pump-out into a shore-based facility. Whether you have a simple portable unit or a top-of-the-line electric system with multiple locations plumbed into a holding tank and utilizing a macerator, you will want to make sure it is properly maintained and cared for.

With smaller boats, the most simple and easy-to-care for unit is the basic portable unit like that of the Thetford Porta Potti 260 or the battery-powered Curve.

As with all similar models in the marine line, this compact system requires only minimal care, including proper replenishing of the deodorizing chemicals and cleaning, to ensure trouble-free operation.

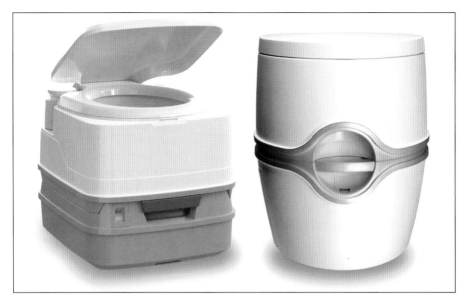

▲ A compact design for smaller boats and versatile enough for larger ones as well, these Thetford models are sure to make your on-water time comfortable for your family and guests. Photo Credit: Thetford

"It's always advisable to keep the slide lock seals between the upper and lower parts properly lubricated as they do tend to wear," said Thetford's Scott Mason. However, as a vessel's length increases, so does its need for a more sophisticated system and in there, to quote the Bard, is the rub.

One of the biggest problems is the result clogging the system by using way too much of the aforementioned t.p. or throwing something down there that, as with your toilet at home, just does not belong. This includes tampons, sanitary napkins, paper towels, and baby wipes. It's best to use toilet paper specifically made for marine use that is both biodegradable and fast dissolving. I'll go out on a limb here by saying that just about every marine store on the planet has a shelf full of the proper product for safe and correct use with your particular unit.

To avoid any problems, many boaters, both new and seasoned, often leave a supply of plastic bags, like those used to clean up after walking the family dog, in the head compartment for disposal of used toilet paper. Pop it in, twist and tie up the bag, and discard on land later. Double bagging just might be necessary.

"The number one trouble maker is using improper tissue," agreed Dometic's Bill Friedman. "Household products are hard to break down, especially going into a pump or with systems using level indicators."

THETF☉RD
Aqua-
SOFT
Toilet Tissue
Specifically for RV and Marine Sanitation Systems

Luxurious
2-PLY
Won't clog drains!

• Rapid-dissolving tissue
• 100% Biodegradable tissue
• Soft, Pure and Snowy White

4 rolls, 184.8 sq. ft. (17.1 sq. m) total area, 2-ply tissue
396 sheets, 4.2 x 4.0 in (10.6 cm x 10.1 cm) per roll

THETF☉RD
RV/MARINE
Toilet Tissue
Quick dissolve tissue recommended for RV/Marine sanitation systems

VALUE
4 ROLL PACK!

• Snowy white 1-ply tissue
• Soft and gentle
• Dissolves quickly
• 100% Biodegradable tissue

4 rolls, 163.3 sq. ft. (15.1 sq. m) total area, 1-ply tissue
350 Sheets, 4.2 in. x 4.0 in. (10.6 cm x 10.1 cm) per roll

▲ Always use marine-grade toilet paper. Photo Credit: Thetford

Okay now, let's not mince words. We're all adults and realize that every living thing, at one time or another during the day will need to eliminate its bodily wastes. And that means odor.

With the removable units, it's merely a matter of disposing of the tank's contents at your marina with a quick and easy pump out each and every time you get back to the dock after a day out. There are many chemical agents and deodorizers you can use on a regular basis as directed by your manufacturer that will keep things not only sanitary but clean smelling as well.

If you have an electrically operated system on your boat, general wear and tear can also be trouble and there is not too much you can do. It's best to keep an eye on things and pay careful attention to your owner's manual for scheduled upkeep. Most of the major manufacturers such as Dometic, Thetford, Headhunter, and Raritan, all have convenient service centers and dealers in the major boating areas.

As far as macerators are concerned, today's units are fairly robust and, but for the errant foreign object (EFO)—again, tampons and sanitary napkins for the most part—forcing an electrical pause and being unable to start up again, you should have uninterrupted service for many years. However, should that EFO find its way into the system, and if you are not the kind who can follow the schematics in your owner's manual, it's time to call in the experts.

▲ Following the manufacturer's directions carefully will result in an odor-free holding tank. Photo Credit: Thetford

Odor and flushing problems on some units can also be caused by a tank vent and filter being clogged by water or debris. Check both of these on a regular basis and make sure you swap out that errant filter according to the manufacturer's recommendations. If so equipped, you might want to consider having a year end cleaning of your holding tank as sediment can settle on the bottom and build up over time.

"To help keep the tank somewhat clean, send a couple of capfuls of liquid laundry detergent into your holding tank, fill it with water, take a ride to slosh things around a bit, and then do a proper pump out at your marina," offered Friedman. "Doing this on a regular basis will be of great help."

Your best bet in preventing problems with your marine toilet is to make sure everyone aboard knows how to properly operate the system and what does, and does not, belong in it. Check all hoses and connections for leaks and try to keep your holding tanks relatively empty whenever possible. In this way, you will have one less thing to worry about while enjoying being on your boat.

Now that we're done with that, let's have a look at what powers your boat through the water.

4. Engines

"I just loved going fast. So I started out with Alka-Seltzer and soda water in a bottle and attached it to the skateboard. That didn't do much. I would try a leaf blower. I was searching for anything that would go fast. Then, the lawnmower engine."

–Kellan Lutz, Actor

The history of the internal combustion engine has a long and memorable lineage that apparently dates back to the third century with a crude apparatus offering the ability to put a crank and connecting rod gizmo to work in a Roman sawmill in Asia Minor—what is today's Turkey.

While that dubiously noted ancestor—whose several spinoff products could very well have resulted in a rudimentary archetype of what would become the toothpick—might not have had the proper genes to set engineers on the path to subsequent experiments, precursors, failures, successes, prototypes, working models, and actual fuel-driven engines, it did illustrate the ability to get work done with this type of machine. It would just be a matter of time and human ingenuity to make it happen for real.

While a contentious debate continues about who actually invented the practical internal combustion engine—with apologies for leaving anyone out, among the many names bantered around in this particular lexicon are Frenchman Nicolas Joseph Cugnot, circa 1769, Englishman Samuel Brown, circa 1824, Belgian-born Jean Joseph Etienne Lenoir, circa 1858, Germans Eugen Langen and Nicholas August Otto, circa 1866 (Otto would receive a patent in 1876 for his four-stroke engine), Gottlieb Daimler, Karl Benz, and Wilhelm Daimler, circa 1885, 1886, and 1890 respectively, and of course Dr. Rudolf Diesel, circa.1893. Suffice it to say that if it weren't for the contributions of these and others, the wheels of progress would have still been pulled by horse and oxen instead of a drive train for quite some time.

Today's sophisticated gasoline and diesel engines, both inboard and outboard, are state-of-the-art, computer controlled, and highly technical machines. Therefore, it is very unlikely, but for some preventative and basic maintenance, that you will be doing any kind of work on them. Knowing the basics is very important and can drastically cut down the odds of things going south, ruining your time out on the water, and costing you lots of money.

The Outboards

You all know the story about how the first practical outboard engine was invented, right? Well if not, it goes something like this:

Ole Andreassen Aaslundeie, was born in 1877 in Oppland, Norway. His father emigrated to the U.S. in 1881, settling in Cambridge, Wisconsin. A year later, Ole, his two siblings, and mother joined him as they worked a family farm near Ripley Lake. Once settled into their new life, their last name became Evinrude—obviously indicating where this little anecdote is going—after Mrs. Aaslundeie's home on Evenrud farm in Vestre Toten, Norway, where she was born.

▲ Ole Evinrude with the outboard engine that would bear his name and change the nature of boating.
Photo Credit: Evinrude

While in his teens, Ole took a job in a machine shop in Madison, Wisconsin, and fascinated with all things motorized and power-driven, taught himself the basics of engineering and mechanical principles.

By 1900, the ambitious Evinrude became a partner in a custom engine company. A mere seven years later came the flywheel cranked, vertical shafted, bevel-geared, steel and brass, two-cycle outboard engine that would revolutionize a design and create an industry.

But there's more to the story than that. The outboard engine was created out of love. Yes, love. You see, as his company grew, so did the need for more employees increase as well. Among them was a young girl by the name of Bessie Cary, who kept the books and, while Ole and his crew tinkered with, built, and repaired their machines in the shop, she tended to most of the company's business end.

Ole was smitten by Bess's good looks as well as her business acumen, and they soon became an item. While on an outing during a summer afternoon in 1906—they would marry later that year—on Milwaukee's Oconomowoc Lake, she expressed a desire for a dish of ice cream. Ole promptly set out to row the distance from their picnic area, some two and a half miles as the story goes, back to shore and fetch the dessert. Of course, by the time he returned, rowing those

▲ A little ice cream and an outboard engine resulted in the birth of an industry for Ole and Bess Evinrude. Photo Credit: Evinrude

same two and a half miles back, the ice cream was quite soupy. But the disappointment he felt at not being able to make Bess happy gave way to an idea that, as with the automobile, a boat could also be powered to move through the water more efficiently and faster than rowing.

In 1911, Ole Evinrude was awarded the patent for his Marine Propulsion Mechanism, also known as the outboard engine. Need we say more?

One last note to this before we move on. During his time at his company, Ole let a young man, also fascinated with motors and engines, spend time in the shop.

His name was Arthur Davidson, and together with his friend, Bill Harley, whom Ole also knew, would go on to found the Milwaukee-based Harley-Davidson Motorcycle Company.

Think about that the next time you enjoy your favorite ice cream.

Today's high-powered, technologically advanced outboards are a far cry from Ole's dessert-saving, 5-hp design. From Seven Marine's behemoth 557-hp giants—truly not for the beginner; nice and impressive to look at but right now, you are a long, long way from considering this kind of power—to those more practical models from Mercury Marine, Yamaha, Suzuki, Evinrude, and Honda among others, the offerings for the first time boater are varied enough to make getting the right power for your boat a rather simple choice.

Mercury Marine

With a product range starting with the 2.5-hp right up through its four-stroke 350-hp Verado, Mercury Marine can match your power needs with your boat of choice. And with its joystick technology, control over your boat equipped with this company's engines has never been easier or more comfortable.

"Think of it this way: it's as if you could take your palm, place it on top of your boat, and be able to move it in any direction you want," said Chris Chapman, Mercury Marine's Application Development Engineer and joystick whiz for the company's outboard engine control project as we spoke about its various applications.

By now, and since the introduction of several joystick control systems over the years, we've become quite used to, and somewhat comfortable with the concept. A twist here. A push there. Dial it around. A short learning curve for newbies and a definite game changer in significantly lowering the pucker factor while in close quarters docking situations or maneuvering. But to have this technology available for use with a pair of outboard engines? Still dubious? Try triple and quad applications as well.

Yes, joystick control is available on outboard engines and when the opportunity to test Mercury Marine's revolutionary system came up aboard a 39-foot Sea Vee center console equipped

▲ As with all engine manufacturers, Mercury has a complete lineup for all applications.

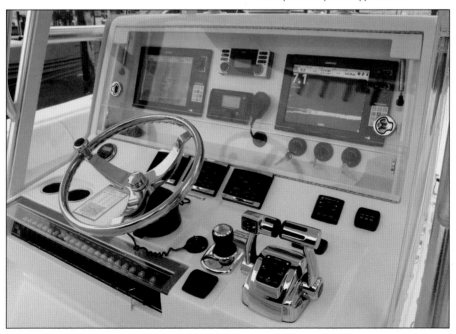

▲ Mercury Marine's joystick is conveniently situated between the wheel and the throttle controls.

▲ If you think Mercury's Joystick Control makes working with a single engine easy, you'll be amazed when you try it with trips.

with triple 300-hp, four-stroke Verado engines came my way, I jumped in with, well, both feet and one hand.

"Our system takes the joystick technology and passes it through the propulsion system," Chapman said as he and I sat at the helm of the test boat. "We have dual and triple applications as well as with quads and multiple stations."

With a smaller Boston Whaler 320 Outrage quietly hovering right outside the dock next to ours, the pair of 300-hp Verados going through their paces while on another demo ride, Chapman led me through the technology and practical applications of the system.

Taking its cues from the advanced and proven systems already in use for larger, diesel powered, pod, and stern driven boats, Mercury has been able to not only make inroads but come up with far-reaching designs in this technology as well. In short, the company has taken the ease of those systems, especially with the simplicity of docking, and given them to outboard engines. It's a definite game changer for those of you who are considering this kind of power for your boat.

Once the domain of hard-core, offshore fishermen, in recent years the center console design has become more popular with families. Indeed, the industry has seen an upswing in these kinds of boats and as I strolled the docks of all the seasonal boat shows, it was obvious that the established, as well as new builders are tailoring their builds and marketing strategies towards family boating.

With Mercury's joystick system you can, with proper instruction and practice, have multiple captains aboard, such as your wife and kids, who, with a much shorter learning curve than that with traditional controls when having to deal with wind and current, are not only capable of getting the boat back to the dock, but will be confident and comfortable with the skill set as well.

"Our engineers have fine-tuned and calibrated the fully integrated system— everything is manufactured by us in one location, from the engines, to the wiring harnesses and rigging, to the controls and autopilot—to a point where we can match the technology to the specific application necessary as pertains to the weight of a certain model of boat where the amount of thrust may not be needed," Chapman said. In other words, heavy boats more and lighter boats less. Translation for you? Ease and confidence with just the right touch.

In developing its outboard joystick controls, Mercury took its cues from both its own internal pulse and that of the consumer. Noting the uptick rate in its successful Axius System—for its inboard, stern drive, and diesel engines—the engineers set their sights on moving the technology across all of the company's product lines.

The sophisticated system has three control modules per engine; an engine control module that manages all of the core engine functions; a thrust vector module, responsible for all the steering functions; and lastly, a helm command and control module.

When in operation, the system takes all its commands from the helm and transfers them for seamless and instantaneous response, telling the engine where it needs to steer and where it needs to be throttling and shifting.

Engaging the joystick control, you can completely and proportionally adjust to any point in between; if you want to go to starboard, merely press slightly in that direction and that engine will shift in reverse with the port going in forward as both splay out. In that way, the direction of the thrust will be directed under the center of gravity beneath the boat. If you need to add a little forward movement, merely push the joystick in that direction. The same goes for reverse, as there is no need at any time to come back to center. It's that easy to continue adding those partial movements to keep things very fluid and maintain control over the boat's momentum so as not to have to regain any motion as the boat moves into the dock.

With the triple engine application, as on my test boat, the center engine will follow whichever engine is in reverse. So for a starboard movement, for example, where the starboard outside engine is in reverse, the center one will swing over and maintain the same angle and assist in reverse. And regardless of dual or triple engines, should the wind get your bow and momentarily put the boat out of shape, a mere twist of the control in the opposite direction will get things back on an even keel very quickly.

That hand-on-the-top-of-your-boat analogy of Chapman's rings true when trying it out for the first time. The initial reaction is how immediate the response is to the command and how, when you first get your hand on the joystick, there is a tendency to twist too much and push too far.

Looking aft and seeing those three 300-hp Verado engines hanging off the transom can be a bit intimidating. But very quickly, and with a bit of practice, the "feel" for things settles in and quite soon after that, your confidence and proficiency with the system will astound you.

As we discussed the experience, Chapman backed up my reaction. "This is a real, intuitive way to move around the dock. With traditional throttle operation, there is usually a lot of movement to jockey into the correct position. Using this system, all that is eliminated. For a non-boater, someone unfamiliar with bringing a boat back in to a dock, we can usually have them comfortable after and hour or so of instruction and practice."

The system also includes an auto trim feature. When coming down off plane from running, you usually tuck the drives back down to minimize the bow rise. What the joystick does, as soon as it is touched, is take that fully tucked trim position and trims the engines back out to a factory preset point so that they are mostly level with the bottom of the boat.

Now let me back up a bit here with a short discussion on the subject of what it means to have a boat equipped with outboard engines properly trimmed out.

The physics of propelling a boat through the water is quite complex with many factors affecting the overall experience including its design, weight, function and the shape and features of its running bottom. With that said, let's limit the conversation to two of those factors, that being fuel efficiency and being able to supply a comfortable and safe ride in the existing sea conditions.

For the most part, outboard engines that are over 30-hp are equipped with an automatic trim and tilt feature. This allows you to adjust the angle of the engine while it is under power—trim—and clear it up out of the water when done for the day—tilt. Being able to perform these operations is accomplished by pressing the buttons usually found on your control head or on either side of your throttles. In the end, this allows you to find your boat's "sweet spot," where it is riding comfortably as per the existing sea conditions as well as enjoying the proper fuel consumption.

Furthering the joystick experience, there are several high-tech options available including a fully integrated Mercury autopilot with waypoint sequencing so you can easily chart your course. Other premium features include a control pad for activating any of the joystick features and Skyhook, Mercury's patented "hovering" system.

Activating it will keep your boat in place against wind and current or while waiting for a spot to open at the fuel dock. It can also be used to get you together while shaping up for docking maneuvers and is a real advantage to offshore fishermen as well with no need to try and anchor in deep water or move off a wreck site where the bite is on.

The VesselView feature allows accessing and monitoring of all your boat's systems as well as being able to set the cruise control. And finally there is Auto Heading, which links its electronic compass onto the boat's heading, keeping it on course with one degree adjustments available from the joystick and 10 degree tuning from the control panel.

One bit of redundancy that is built into the system covers a rather familiar scenario and one that none of us want to deal with while away from the dock.

Given the amount of electronics we have become used to using all the time—chartplotter, radar, sounder, radio, entertainment center, baitwell pump, lights, phone chargers, and lots of other electric gear—a situation might arise where there is a depletion of your cranking batteries' power.

If the Mercury system identifies this is happening, it will automatically raise the idle rate of the engines and bring the charge current up. Other features

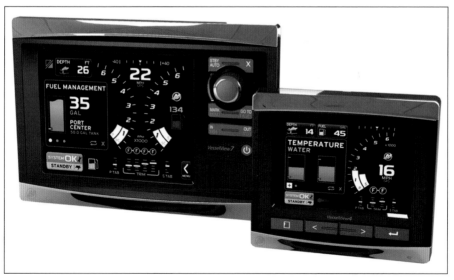

▲ Available in standard 4-inch LCD screen, or optional 6.4-inch touchscreen, VesselView lets you access all critical data quickly and effortlessly. Photo Credit: Mercury Marine

include one power steering pump and one steering cylinder per engine just in case there is a problem with any other engine. There is also a guardian mode that will kick in so as not to allow the engine to operate outside of accepted parameters. And there are anti-collision cables between all multiple engine applications.

Mercury Marine's R&D was as focused and determined with this technology as it has been in the past when bringing other new advances forward. "We've had multiple validation cycles and tests, punishing the product way before we brought it to the consumer level," Chapman said. With everything I've seen and experienced, the company has done its homework. The result is a user-friendly system that brings a new level of comfort to the outboard sector and one that just might get those on the fence about handling a boat down off it and onto the deck and at the helm. There are a host of video productions which can be found on the Mercury Marine Website and for further information, you should check them out.

OTHER SYSTEMS

◀ Sea Star's Optimus 360 can be used across several platforms as well as in retrofits.

While the Mercury system is the only one I actually had my hands on, similar ease-of-control and confidence at the wheel, especially geared up for new boaters, is also available with Yamaha's Helm Master system and Evinrude's ICON iDock and Sea Star Solutions' Optimus 360. And there's even an Optimus 360 retrofit system for those of you who may have decided on a brokerage boat with outboard power.

Let's have a look at some of the other outboard engines on the market from the top manufacturers. All have many warranty plans, options and programs for you to participate in as well as extensive video presentations to make both operations and maintenance that much easier to perform, especially for beginning boaters. There are some great presentations available on YouTube as well. In addition, many engine companies have partnered up with boat manufacturers, such as Yamaha with Grady-White and Evinrude with Larson and Scout, making matching the kind of power you will need for your particular boat that much easier.

Given the competition for your business, no matter which engine you choose for your new boat, these manufacturers are dedicated to assisting you in any way they can including setting up test rides on various boats. Should you wish to see all the offerings from any of these companies, please visit their websites.

Yamaha

This highly respected engine manufacturer has a complete lineup of models to suit any need. From its 350-hp, 5.3L four-stroke V8 to its somewhat more tamer 250-hp, 3.3L four-stroke V6, and to quite a few more, Yamaha has been hanging on transoms for over thirty years now and has garnered a stellar reputation for clean burning, fuel efficient, and dependable service. www.yamahaoutboards.com

▲ Photo Credit: Yamaha

Evinrude

With its aforementioned historical significance in the industry, Evinrude has gone through several iterations throughout the years and has recently introduced not only a new line of engines but also an entirely new look for the twenty-first century as well.

The company offers a complete lineup of engines from 3.5-hp right through a high performance lineup spanning 15- to 250-hp, its 150- to 300-hp V6's, and on up to its G2 200-hp to 300-hp, also available in nine color combinations. www.evinrude.com

▲ Photo Credit: Evinrude

Honda

Honda entered the outboard market with four-stroke technology and has continued with that mission ever since. With a complete lineup starting with its 2.3- to 20-hp portables, its 25- to 100-hp mid range motors, and right up to its high power engines starting with a 115-hp offering to the top-of-the-line BF

250-hp, all Honda outboards have a long list of standard and optional features.

The company also covers all new engines with its True 5 Year Limited Warranty against any defects in materials or workmanship from the date of purchase. According to Honda, this is not an extended warranty nor is it non-declining—not pro-rated or decreased as the end date approaches—and is fully transferable should you decide to sell your boat, and with over one thousand dealer centers throughout the U.S., getting service will not be a problem. www.hondamarine.com

▲ Photo Credit: Honda Marine

Suzuki

Committing itself to developing four-stroke technology across its offerings in the outboard engine sector, Suzuki has an extensive model lineup with which to match to the boat of your choice.

Starting with a 2.5-hp portable and right on up to a 4L, 300-hp V6 powerhouse, the company has an equally long list of accessories, optional color display for your instrument panel, gauges, engine covers, and warranty information. www.suzukimarine.com

▲ Photo Credit: Suzuki Marine

The Inboards

Given you are not starting with a larger boat, you will most likely end up with outboard power. However, there are some inboard engine manufacturers that have powerplants that are quite suitable for some entry-level boats.

We'll begin with the inboard/outboard, also known as the I/O or stern drive. One of the more interesting engine designs, this mating of inboard and outboard, was the brainchild of engineering whiz kid Jim Wynne back in the late 1950s.

Wynne, who together with fellow engineer Charlie Strang, worked at Mercury under the tyrannical reign of larger-than-life company founder Carl Kiekhaefer—if you want some great background reading and some insight into the man and the empire he forged, get a copy of *Iron Fist: The Lives of Carl Kiekhaefer* by Jeffrey L. Rodengen. It's an eye opening page-turner to be sure.

While there are conflicting stories of who actually was the architect of its development, especially between both visionary engineers Strang and Wynne, by the time the latter left Mercury in 1957, after Kiekhaefer did not support the idea of a stern drive, he set out on his own. Undaunted, and with plenty of time on his hands, he began tinkering with a design using a Penta BB70 inboard engine.

After a trip to Denmark, he dropped into the Göteborg, Sweden, headquarters of Volvo Penta, showed them his design papers and sketches and, as the story goes, two days later, Jim Wynne was handed a contract.

The Volvo Penta Aquamatic Stern Drive engine made its world appearance at the 1959 New York Boat Show to rave reviews. And the rest is history.

There must have been a rather satisfying moment, I would imagine, from Wynne's then-vantage point to this bit of nautical history: in 1961, after initially dismissing his former engineer's idea, Kiekhaefer and Mercury Marine introduced the MerCruiser stern drive engine.

At its simplest, a stern drive has the engine, offering more horsepower than an outboard, mounted aft and inside the boat with its highly maneuverable linkage and prop sticking out the aft end.

Without the clutter of hanging a large motor off the transom, the area is now clear. Some boat builders prefer this application as they now do not have to design prop shafts, struts, and rudders into those models using stern drive propulsion.

No one system is perfect and of concern, of course, is that the lower unit is open to hitting submerged objects, catching debris, or smacking that errant piece of wood you didn't see. While any gear can be damaged in this way—I've dinged a prop or two in my career running a traditional inboard powered boat with shafts and struts, touched bottom now and then, and picked up plenty of fishing and polypropylene line that wound its way up the shaft and into the cutlass bearings—still, there may be a bit more in the water with an I/O. Stern drive engines are available in both gasoline and diesel models.

▲ Revolutionary in design, the Volvo Penta Aquamatic married an outboard with an inboard engine. Photo Credit: Volvo Penta

As long as we've mentioned it, long the backbone and workhorse of both the on-road and marine industries, the diesel engine has proven to be the preferred standard for inboard power.

While there were many designs, prototypes, archetypes and working models that contributed to its development, it was most likely the work of Dr. Rudolf Diesel—hence its name—that brought this dependable workhorse of an engine into prominence.

Diesel received a patent for his invention, known as a compression ignition engine, in February of 1892. Without the need for a traditional ignition system, the Diesel engine, after bringing its fuel in—yes, peanut or vegetable oil—and introducing it into a cylinder that had compressed air to a very high degree, the oil, in the presence of the extreme heat of the air, is ignited in a controlled explosion.

Diesel's economical power was far more efficient than the energy-wasting steam engines of the times and by 1912, was being used for all sorts of factory and generator applications. They would soon revolutionize the railroad, truck, and bus industries, and eventually become marinized for ship, yacht, and boat use.

Today's computerized-controlled energy compliant engines are a far cry from those of Dr. Diesel's day but they still retain the efficiency and ability to deliver the grueling demands of modern technology that was built into those early models.

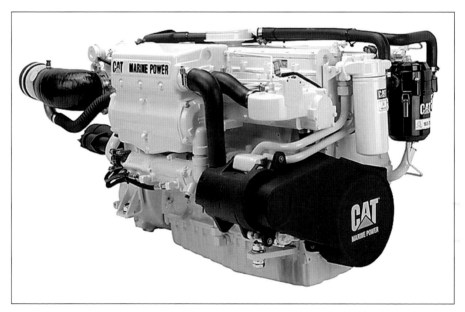

▲ Today's modern diesel engines are computer controlled with systems designed for maximum power and efficiency along with complying with environmental standards for clean operation. Photo Credit: Caterpillar

With advanced designs and systems from such noteworthy engine manufacturers as MAN, Cummins, MTU, Volvo Penta, Caterpillar, Yanmar, John Deere, and others, there is a diesel-powered engine for almost every inboard marine application.

Gasoline inboards are yet another option. Unlike a diesel, which compresses air to high temperatures and then delivers a fine plume of fuel for ignition, a gasoline engine, much like the one in your car, uses spark plugs to ignite the gasoline and put it into play. It also needs a carburetor to mix the air and fuel into a highly combustible mixture while controlling the ratio of that blend as well.

There has always been a back and forth conversation on the pros and cons of each; noisier, heavier, more expensive diesels with less fuel-efficient but lighter weight gasoline engines are among some of the many talking points.

▲ With advanced systems and monitoring, gasoline inboards, such as Mercury Marine's MerCruiser lineup, offer a complete performance package. Photo Credit: Mercury Marine

When making the choice for inboard power, it's a good idea to discuss how you are going to use your boat with your dealer in order to help determine which kind of engine is going to serve you best. Again, with today's technologically advanced designs and superior, safe systems, having gasoline inboards just might help with your finances.

Before we move on, we need to have a look at something really different. It is the kind of technology that truly changed the way boaters, and especially entry-level, prospective owners, were given the opportunity to have the kind of control over their boats that promised, and delivered, to take the anxiety of docking, as well as being in close quarters situations, out of the equation.

In retrospect, and just like the new joystick controls for outboard engines we already discussed, it would serve to bring new boaters, those who could never see themselves in control of a boat, into the lifestyle with an ease and comfort level as yet unimagined.

If you've spent the past years since its introduction in 2004 under a rock or have been lost in the jungle wilds of New Guinea and just returned to civilization, you need to have a look at Volvo Penta's Inboard Performance System, better known by is acronymic IPS.

I was at the world introduction for the IPS at Volvo Penta headquarters in Göteborg, Sweden, back then—same place where Jim Wynne made his

▲ Volvo Penta's IPS system has added a new dimension to boat handling, especially for new boaters.
Photo Credit: Volvo Penta

Aquamatic stern drive deal—and by the time I got through the introduction and Q&A with all the designers, engineers, and upper level executives responsible for this new system, pods with forward facing props, I couldn't wait to get down to the docks, to the test boats, and give it a whirl.

The experience was eye opening. With three pair of boats from the same builder in different size configurations, one was outfitted with IPS drives and the other with conventional shaft and prop. All the boats were loaded with the same fuel and water capacity as well as persons aboard and were as close to being identical as possible. In this way, we would be able to make side-by-side, apples-to-apples comparisons.

Faster acceleration, a quieter ride, better fuel economy, agility and responsiveness with the kind of maneuverability akin to driving a hot sports car, and real speed out of the hole as compared to being at the wheel of the other boats.

Today's IPS drives can be found on boats from 30-feet up to 100-feet, from entry-level boats to sport fishing boats, to big cruising yachts, in single as well as multi-engine configurations. And with electronic joystick controls, docking maneuvers are a piece of cake. Seven-layer cake.

Basic Engine Maintenance

It's most likely unnecessary for you to become a master mechanic; after all, whether you have an outboard, I/O, or diesel or gasoline inboard, and as we've made the point, your engine is a sophisticated, computer controlled machine whose functions are, for all practical purposes, and unless you are a schooled and trained mechanic and technician, way beyond your skill level.

However, there are some fundamental tasks, sure to be gone over during your dealer tutorial, that you are quite capable of taking on in order to maintain your equipment and make sure it is running well. With that in mind, let's look at some hands-on preventive maintenance items that should become part of your daily and regularly scheduled regimen.

▶ As you can readily see, today's outboard engines are complex machines that require expert technical attention. Photo Credit: Mercury Marine

First off, it is extremely important to read and become familiar with your owner's manual. This will give you all the information you will need, including identifying and locating such important items as oil and fuel filters, coolant reservoirs, dip sticks, fuel and water pumps, belts, and other areas you will be dealing with. In addition, there are many quality, well produced, informative, and highly descriptive how-to videos on the Internet, including the individual engine manufacturers and YouTube, that will show you, step by step, exactly what you are looking for and how to do it. I highly recommend spending some time with these kinds of presentations as telling you about it and seeing it are two very different things.

Whether with outboard, inboard gasoline or diesel, or I/O engine operation, one of the most important things you can do is to check your oil each and every time you take your boat out. The only thing keeping your machinery from experiencing a catastrophic break down is a thin film of oil.

It is extremely important to know the acceptable operational levels such as water temperature, oil pressure, and the proper lube levels at which your engine operates. Pay special attention to making sure when you change oil and filters, you do so at the same time and always according to the manufacturers recommendations and timetable as per engine hours.

Use only that specific to your engine and do not, under any circumstances go to Discount Harry's Second Hand Auto Parts & Lawn Furniture Store for this. And please, put down oil absorbent pads under the engine, use a funnel when adding, and be sure to wipe up any residue you may spill.

Some engines can go quite a while until a required maintenance is due while others need to be addressed on a tighter schedule. And whenever doing oil, oil and fuel filter changes, or any other kind of maintenance, remember to note this in your boat's log. It will be of invaluable help to you as you begin to put hours on your engines and assist you in staying on track with this important information.

With that said, let's start with the inboard systems that need to be attended. First, when opening the engine room deck hatch, make sure it is secured and will not suddenly come down on you. A smack on the head from a rapidly closing hatch cover can do some damage.

Have a rag or several paper towels at the ready and locate the oil dipstick. Pull it out, wipe it clean, and reinsert it. Wait a moment or two before removing it and noting the oil level.

If oil needs to be added, put in only enough to hit the proper mark on the stick. Also, it's a good idea to note the oil's color; very dark or black usually indicates it's time for new oil. Check your owner's manual for recommended change times.

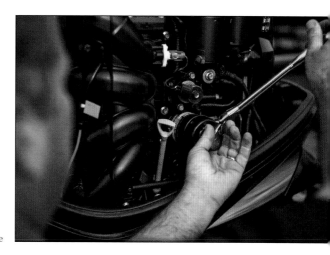

▶ The yellow oil dipstick is clearly marked and easily reached for checking fluid levels. Photo Credit: Mercury Marine

Next, locate the coolant cap. Using a small flashlight, unscrew the cap and have a look at the fluid level; it should be visible. A fingertip dipped inside should come up wet. Again, if you need to add any coolant, do so with the proper product.

Another area to check is the transmission fluid level—if the usually pinkish liquid appears milky white do not start your engine. You have water infiltration and will need to get the mechanics in post haste—and any belts for your alternator or water pump; merely run your finger along the inside area. If any teeth are missing, or with a visual inspection, you see any nicks or gouges, replace it immediately. On this note, you should be carrying spare belts and enough oil, oil and fuel filters, and coolant to do one complete change should that be necessary.

Always note the flow of exhaust water. If you see a decrease in the output, shut down as you may have a blockage; perhaps you sucked up a plastic bag or some other debris. It could also be a faulty impeller within the water pump. If so, the only way to tell is to open up the inspection plate on the pump and have a look at the impeller blades. If any are compromised, a new one will need to be installed. It's a good idea to carry a spare one of these as well.

Besides visually inspecting all hoses, clamps, and through hull connections, as well as the air filters and Racor fuel water separators, there's not too much else you are going to be able to do at this point. It's most likely prudent to first hire your basic maintenance jobs out in the beginning when you need anything done and carefully observe, participate, and ask questions as your dock mates and marina service manager assist. Once you see it happen, you will be able to do it on your own. Again, there are many excellent video tutorials on YouTube as well as on individual engine sites. The learning curve

▲ From left to right, impellers in various stages of failure. The one on the far right is a new one.

is not steep at all and once mastered, it is quite rewarding to DIY. (That's do-it-yourself, by the way.)

On the outboard side, and as with any engine, always follow the manufacturer's recommendations as per your owner's manual, especially as your new equipment will be under warranty.

Starting with checking the oil level, you can get it done while the boat is in the water. However, when you need that first and subsequent oil changes, and as this requires draining, it's best to be on land.

The first thing to do is tilt the motor up and out of the water for about two to three minutes, this to move any oil that might be in the power head forward and, once tilted back down, into the reservoir below.

Remove the cowling and locate the oil dipstick. Check the level and if within accepted limits, you can replace it and move on to the next inspection point. On some engines, the dipstick locks in and once you are done, it will need to be clicked back into place.

One of the more important maintenance tasks you can do on your new outboard engine is to flush it out with fresh water after each use. There is no need to run the engine as most will be equipped with a built-in flushing device that can usually be found near the rear of the cowling.

By merely hooking up your dockside hose and lifting the lower unit up out of the water, or if you trailer, to your garden hose when you get home, once you turn on the tap, let the water run for about ten minutes or so after which you can disconnect the hose, making sure the cap is replaced on the flush fitting.

This procedure helps to prevent any saltwater corrosion—freshwater users are urged to perform this after each and every use as well—from taking root and removes any sediment or debris that might have found its way up into the cooling system. If you keep your boat in a slip in a marina and are done for the day, tilt your engine up out of the water until you are ready to go out again. Again, there are some great video presentations to show you how to do this very simple preventive maintenance procedure. Type in "fresh water outboard flushing" in your search window and you will get lots of visual aids.

The "sniff test" requires you to be aware of any errant gasoline smell. Should even a hint be present, get everyone off the boat and do not start your engine. Instead, carefully check all fuel system components for leaks. If you do not discover any, and there is still that pervasive and highly recognizable odor, call in your marina manager for their expertise. As a new boater, you might be missing something that someone with the knowledge and background with this kind of issue will know where to look.

Should everything check out, make sure you have enough fuel for your time away from the dock and top off your fuel tank before setting out for the day.

Other areas to get a visual on are the condition of the prop, making sure your tilt and trim operates properly, and making certain that your scuppers, bilge areas, and drains are all clean and clear of any debris. And always, double check if your drain plug is installed and secure if so equipped. Again, you will get a complete rundown from your dealership on all phases of your boat's operations.

As with most information gathering today, there are many, many online sites where you will be able to find excellent instructional videos that will lead you, step by step, along with clear-cut visuals on just about anything you may need to get the job done. I have found that merely putting in a key word will get you connected to a host of first-rate industry experts. Using this kind of access will definitely be of value, as you get more and more comfortable with your boat and its systems.

A NOTE ON FUEL ADDITIVES

Before we move on to another topic, let's wrap things up here with a discussion on fuel additives. Since there has always been a lot of conversation on this matter, let's get a few basic facts down before we open up the fuel fill and dump some mystic conditioning brew into our tanks.

Oil, the result of the detritus of once living organisms, has spent millions of years "cooking" under intense pressure beneath both land and sea. Fast-forward a couple of thousand epochs, eras, and millennia . . . well, you get the idea, to when the first oil well finally popped the cork.

It's a dirty business getting the dirty product refined and to market in its many forms to run the world as we know it. During the refining process at those expansive plants with their cloud-spewing towers, seemingly miles of above ground pipes, and fields of storage tanks, the crude oil is processed into the lifeblood of just about everything we use in our everyday lives. And, among all the other products that come out of the spigot, there is the stuff that we are most concerned with: gasoline and diesel fuel.

The problem, and the reason why you might want to use a fuel additive or conditioner, begins with the refining process. "Because the refiners are trying to get as much out of a barrel of crude that they can, today's aggressive process of splitting open the molecules, using catalysts and high temperatures is far different that the distilling methods of years ago, and can create more instability in the after products," said Barry Sprague, as we discussed the matter. Sprague is a chemist and consultant to NJ-based Technol Fuel Conditioners (www.technol.com).

But wait, as said in those obnoxious infomercials, there's more! Moving downstream from the refining process are a host of ills waiting to be visited upon our precious gasoline and diesel fuel.

For example, with those of you who use gasoline in your inboard and outboard engines, the government-mandated fuel contains oxygenated additives, offshoots of methyl and ethyl alcohol. Add some heat and moisture along with the sometimes lengthy storage time the gasoline is sitting around, from refinery tanks to tanker trucks to your marina tanks, and not only are you liable to get less efficient fuel but a bit on the dirty side as well.

"With those who run gasoline engines, you might want to consider a treatment with every oil change," said Sprague. "You really want to help control that moisture as the alcohol can separate out with only the minimal amount of water."

For diesel fuel oil, and along with the same issues associated with gasoline storage, there are the low sulfur levels—also courtesy of the EPA—combined with the products' affinity for water, sludge, and bio-growth (bacteria and fungi), that can also present problems. "What we want to do here is even out the playing field for performance, how the fuel is handled once it gets to the end user in regards to its stability, and trying to control any contaminants," said Sprague.

So, here's where our additives, stabilizers, treatments, and conditioners come into play. The first thing you want to do is keep a careful watch on your primary and secondary fuel filters. If you are so equipped, drain your Racors or similar systems should any sign of water be present. If you have to change the elements

▲ Before using any fuel additive, check with your engine manufacturer on their recommendations.

a bit more often, or if you begin to notice a drop in rpm levels, you more than likely have a fair amount of gunk in your tanks that is getting roiled up as you use your boat and is clogging the free flow of fuel to the engine(s).

"With severe problems in this area, such as obvious plugging, and more usually found in older boats, it's best to take some time out and have those fuel tanks professionally cleaned," suggested Sprague.

For you diesel users, this filter problem can be a direct result of using a biocide additive. As the juice begins to do its work and kill the "bugs" at the water/oil interface, which is where the organisms live, the accumulated buildup will be added to the already sludgy bottom layer of the fuel tank resulting in a totally non-combustible mass getting sucked up into the fuel system. "If you think you might have something growing, you should use a biocide treatment but be aware of the consequences," offered Sprague. Again, new boat owners needn't worry too much about this . . . for now.

Fuel stabilizers do their work by scavenging and removing oxygen that may get into the fuel by several means including the ever-present motion and agitation as the boat moves through the water. "Even trace amounts of oxygen present in the fuel can cause problems," said Sprague.

To simplify the chemistry, the additive can help repair the hydrocarbon chain that was "damaged" at the refinery and/or chemically remove most of the trace oxygen making it more stable and therefore, more efficient. They also work to emulsify, or blend, any water droplets present in the fuel oil thus helping to impede the growth of bacteria. Other positive results include breaking down of particulate matter that can be safety filtered out, and the shattering of larger contaminants that can be burned off during combustion.

However, there is a *caveat emptor* attached to using any fuel additive: make sure you check with your engine manufacturer before adding any of these products to your tanks as they can void a warranty that is currently in effect. In addition, many engine manufacturers offer a recommended product line, or their own, for use with their power plants and fuel systems. And as with any product such as additives, always follow the directions on the container or bottle as to the correct amounts that need to be added per gallon. Should you have any questions, do not hesitate to contact the manufacturer.

With today's highly advanced engines, and because of the aggressive refinery processes that result in a more unstable end product, using a fuel treatment can help you get the best possible grade of gasoline or diesel fuel into your system and have you running more efficiently with the added result of a positive effect on the environment.

A NAUTICAL ASIDE

The way Capt. Ryan Clark looks at things goes something like this: *"Maybe one day, when it's time, I'll go somewhere carrying around an anchor in my car. When I get to that place where someone says, 'Hey, what's that?' well I just might settle down there. Then again . . ."*

5. Running Gear: Props, Shafts, and Struts

"Eureka! I have found it!"

–Archimedes, Greek Mathematician, Physicist, Engineer, Inventor,
Astronomer, Considered the Father of The Screw Propeller

*Y*ears back—and that would be many years back—I had a license to six-pack my 42-foot, Maine-built, wood Downeast lobster boat to help offset some college expenses and put a bit of beer money in my pocket. That limited me to no more than six passengers aboard to fish, and I gave them their money's worth. I frequently caught a propeller blade on debris. This led me to have to pull the single prop and have a go at it, Fred Flintstone-like, to try and hammer out the ding as best I could. A day off the water for me could mean a serious snafu in my economic status.

Slapping the prop back on, I often found I had gotten it in shape enough to not feel any undue vibration and still able to make my usual eight knots courtesy of a very reliable six cylinder, 90-hp Ford Lehman flat head diesel. Nine knots with a fair tide.

Knowing full well this could only be a Band-Aid fix—and not a smart one at that—I promptly went out and got a fairly good spare, spun the old one off, slapped the new one on, and sent the damaged goods off to be done up the right way.

Long gone are those years. Today's props are as finely designed, built, and tuned as one of Stradivarius's violins. And for good reason.

As engine design, both on the outboard and inboard side, has gotten more sophisticated, so has the need to match the correct prop to the overall efficiency of the entire package. Parameters such as fuel economy, vibration—a real big factor—and speed can be affected.

Propeller manufacturers use sophisticated computer programs to not only design the most efficient ones to match your boat and engine, but have extensive and detailed data bases to equal either a spare, a repair, or a replacement should that be necessary.

You most probably have heard the terms diameter and pitch spoken about when discussing props. The former is the distance measured from the hub, that is the center of the prop to the outer tip of a blade. You then double that measurement to get the total diameter of the prop. Pitch is described as the distance covered, measured in inches, for one complete revolution of the prop as it moves forward through the water. Pitch is an important factor in overall engine performance. A boat with a propeller whose pitch is too high might increase speed, but if the engine does not have enough horsepower to keep it running in the optimum rpm range, overall performance will be affected and damage to the engine is a real possibility.

For the inboard boat owner, your running gear—that is, your prop and struts, which hold the shaft securely to the bottom of the boat—and rudders all work together as seamlessly as possible. Should anything happen, such as hitting a piece of wood or running aground, and let's say your prop gets dinged, you bend a strut, or from the stress, the integrity of the hull is compromised, big trouble can and will ensue.

For example, with a damaged prop, even the slightest vibration can cause a rippling effect that will travel through the shaft and up to the transmission coupling. Not good. The bearings that hold the shaft in the struts can wear down quickly to a point where the shaft is now scored and may have to be replaced or machined to make it viable.

On the subject of damaged props, and for those that are not beyond repair, they can be brought back using a sophisticated computer program. Placing the prop on a spinning table and taking finite measurements across each blade, the values are then compared to those of the original design. Once that is done, trained and skilled workers can re-tune the prop back.

One of the major players in this particular high-tech sector is Prop Scan (www. propscanusa.com). With its ability to get highly accurate readings, such problems as vibration, engine overload, proper synchronization for twin-engine applications, excessive fuel consumption, and other prop-related issues can be resolved.

For outboard and I/O equipped boats, and while there is no running gear, still, the lower unit is open to damage and should that happen, more than the prop will need to be repaired and possibly replaced.

▲ A properly designed and tuned propeller can mean better performance, improved fuel economy, and a smooth, vibration free ride.

Again, with today's understanding and advanced technology, engine manufacturers, boat builders, and prop and running gear companies possess the kind of information to match these critical components to your particular boat with a very high degree of accuracy. They all need to work together to give you the safest and most efficient time out on the water and whether inboard or outboard power is used on your boat, rest assured that when you take delivery, everything will be in harmony. It's up to you to keep it that way.

6. Electronics

"I may not have gone where I intended to go, but I think I have ended up where I needed to be."

—*Douglas Adams, Writer*

*J*ust as advances in electronic controls, computerized engines, and even boat-building design and techniques have revolutionized the industry and therefore, your enjoyment of the boating lifestyle, so has technology enabled consumer marine electronics to be so far advanced in both ease of use and accuracy that they have become standard packages on even the smallest of entry-level boats.

GPS

As a first-time boater, you most likely have little or no experience with nautical navigation techniques. However, if you've used a GPS in your car, or via any of the direction assisting apps available on your smartphone, the learning curve for marine electronics will be a lot less than you imagined.

So, let's start with GPS, a term that has become part of the language of everyday conversation. The letters stand for **G**lobal **P**ositioning **S**ystem, and like most advanced electronic systems it was first developed for highly sensitive military applications for the Department of Defense. Once the technology was declassified, it found its way into the public consumer sector, into our cars, our phones, our watches, and onto the helms of our boats.

▲ This compact Raymarine multifunction display unit mounts easily at the helm. With touch control, a bright screen, and the ability to be expandable as your needs grow with experience, this powerful navigation unit will get you there and back. Photo Credit: Raymarine

With the equipment and prevalence so widespread, and entry-level price point within easy reach, GPS receivers—so called because that helm-mounted unit, once activated, is getting signals from a collection of satellites in Earth's orbit—have become an indispensable component of the total boating experience and add a high degree of safety and confidence while underway with easily operated yet sophisticated navigation abilities.

If you were ever intimidated by trying to understand or operate these kinds of electronics, let your fears be put aside. All of the entry-level units on the market today are extremely user-friendly and with just the basic, hands-on tutorials, both conceptualizing and realizing the abilities these powerful machines have along with your comfort level with all the various operations, will be easily achieved.

GPS works by using a series of satellites—by last count it was some twenty-seven with three backups ready to be put into service in case there is a problem with any of the others—in arranged orbits, each making two complete fly-bys in a twenty-four-hour period at about twelve thousand miles up, so that at least four of them are able to be seen at any time and anywhere around the globe. Although by chance, and by using a really good, high-powered telescope, you might be able to glimpse a view of one as it zips across the sky. (For this conversation, by "seen" I mean by the now powered-up GPS receiver.)

Cutting to the chase here, your unit will then locate at least three or more of the satellites and with its sophisticated inner electronics, decode the information, including the distance between you and the satellites, and tell you, more or less, and along with lots of other information, precisely where you are on a brilliantly lit, and very detailed, electronic chart right there on the display. How exact? Try twenty to forty feet from your GPS receiver.

Don't even try to think about the mathematics, or the physics, or the advanced technology, or the concept of radio waves—but a neat factoid is as they travel at the astounding rate of the speed of light, that being 186,000 miles per second, your GPS receiver can, in less than an instant, figure out the distance that signal has traveled by actually timing how long it took to get to your unit's location—that makes all this possible. Instead, be confident and safe in the thought that when you power it up, it works and works really well. This is as bulletproof as entry-level, advanced electronics gets.

With this information in hand, and before we have a look at the most popular units on the market for entry-level boaters, please take the following thought into consideration. While I was doing my research for this section, I was able to have a look at the latest units. As of this writing, and just like with iPhone and other electronic gizmos, they are quickly being replaced by the next generation of whatever doodad thingy we all just must have.

Some of the features I think you might want to consider in whatever unit you are looking at are touch screen capability—I prefer this feature but the more conventional zoom knob works just fine—flush or bracket mounting—the former always looks the best but only if your helm area has the room—a bright screen that can be easily viewed in sunlight as well as with polarized sunglasses, built-in GPS antenna, anti-fogging construction, ability to link up wirelessly with other devices, and the largest viewing area for your needs.

Garmin

Since its founding in 1989, Garmin has been an industry mainstay in GPS technology. With many entry-level units in its lineup, including chartplotters and combination models, you are sure to find one that will fit your application and helm area.

▲ Photo Credit: Garmin

For example, the 741xs offers a seven-inch color touchscreen display, can be totally integrated with other Garmin products, and, among many other features, is a superfast, accurate machine with a proven track record. www.garmin.com

Furuno

With a long list of innovative developments in electronics going back as far as 1938, Furuno has a wide range of electronic navigation equipment for every budget.

For most beginners, the GP-1870f seven-inch color screen will be the one to get you started. There are many outstanding features with this one and while you may not use them, it's good to know they are there. www.furuno.com

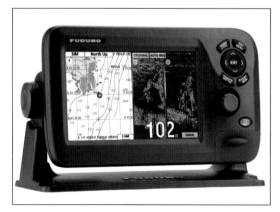

▲ Photo Credit: Furuno

Raymarine

One of the oldest electronic entities in the business, Raymarine began as a company in 1923 and has been a pioneering leader in the industry ever since. Acquired by FLIR in 2010, it continues to provide the latest in technology for the marine industry.

The A Series Touch Screen lineup is available in four models—5.7-, 7-, 9-, and 12" screens. These units feature swipe, touch, and navigate abilities, networking options, and super bright LED displays among many other features, all in an easy-to-use and intuitive package. www.raymarine.com

▲ Photo Credit: Raymarine

Lowrance

With the release of its Little Green Box consumer sonar unit in 1957, Lowrance is a name easily recognizable by boaters looking for quality electronics for fishing and cruising.

▲ Photo Credit: Lowrance

The newest Elite Series features a pair of chartplotters with high-resolution, 5- and 7-inch color screens with lots of features. Its page selector allows quick access to all its functions and multi-window display permits pre-set page layout views, including a three-panel scene, while still having live charting up on the display. www.lowrance.com

Simrad

Simrad began its climb up the consumer electronics ladder in 1946 and the range of offerings covers recreational vessels of all sizes and configurations including sportfishing, cruising, and superyachts.

▲ Photo Credit: Simrad

Simrad has several units in both 5- and 7-inch displays that fit into any beginning boater's needs and budget. From its GO5 XSE plotter and multifunction model to the GO7 XSE, and everything else in between, each of these have outstanding features and many extras and options. www.simrad-yachting.com

VHF Radios

The other piece of must-have electronics is a really good handheld VHF radio. Most likely your boat will already come equipped with a fixed, dash-mounted unit as part of your electronics package. However, I never go anywhere without my portable.

Standard Horizon's HX 870, and ICOM M25

These are among the more popular units from these top companies. Some things to look for are floatability, being waterproof, long battery life, 5 to 6 watts of power, large display, and clear voice among other features. If for the safety factor alone, I would suggest you look into getting a better unit rather than something a bit less in cost. And as with most things aboard, make sure everyone, even the kids, knows how to use it. Visit each company's website for all their offerings.

▲ Photo Credit: Standard Horizon; www.standardhorizon.com

▲ Photo Credit: Icom; www.icomamerica.com

FLIR

You might also want to consider having a FLIR Scout TK up on your helm and at the ready. This handheld, marine thermal camera is a wonderful addition to your navigation equipment. (www.flir.com)

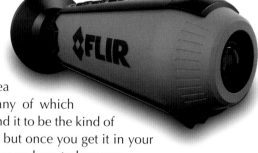
▼ FLIR's Scout TK fits easily in your hand and can come in handy during running in low light or in the evening. Photo Credit: FLIR

I've used one of these during sea trials and other assignments, many of which extended long after dark, and found it to be the kind of gear one doesn't know one needs but once you get it in your hands, you wonder why it took you so long to buy one.

This is just a small overview of the many offerings in this sector. The best advice with all electronic equipment is to give it a test ride at a local dealer or, even better, at a boat show where you can go from booth to booth, from display to display, and get your hands on every device you are interested in. Also, make sure to visit all the company websites and have a look at not only their many offerings, but their online video tutorials as well. Again, we have these resources at a keystroke and it is a wise and prudent boat owner that will take advantage of them.

Before we move on, and as long as we've been discussing electronics, you should be aware of the many apps that are now available to boaters. These can be invaluable not only on the informational side but on the practical as well. Check out such sites as the U.S. Power Squadron (www.usps.org), Boating Magazine (www.boatingmag.com), BoatUS (www.boatus.com), U.S. Coast Guard (www.uscg.mil/mobile/), MarinaLife (www.marinalife.com), and many others. For a more comprehensive search, try your individual electronics manufacturer's site. As well, there are many other apps covering a wide range of varied uses such as security—www.qcampro.com.au and www.gostglobal.com are both excellent resources—travel, maintenance, navigation, first aid, and other topics.

7. Wind, Weather, and Tides

"Climate is what we expect, weather is what we get."
                    —-Mark Twain, American Writer, Humorist, and Lecturer

*C*onsider this: The earth spins at a rate of 1,040 miles per hour, or for you metric folks, at 1,675 kilometers per hour. Let's not even try and break that down to distance per second. Way too much to think about. But wait! There's more! How fast do you think our galaxy is moving?

Well, according to calculations far beyond my pay grade, the arm of the Milky Way that contains our eight, or nine planets as some have stated here on the strong side of a decade and a half plus into the twenty-first century, and all its other various comets, asteroids, meteors, and other contents, we are scooting along at a calculated rate of 140 miles per second, give or take. Whatever. I'm getting a headache just thinking about it. What is equally astounding is the result of all that movement: the weather.

Being new boaters, our discussion is going to concentrate more on recognizing local weather patterns and how to read the sky rather than the complex physics that, for the deep water aficionados, drives our offshore waters and those down past the horizon. I don't think at this point, as you begin your boating experience, you are going to be planning to cross oceans or having to deal with trade winds, gyres, and major global cross currents.

▲ Always pay attention to not only the weather in your area but should you be traveling somewhere, make sure you check the local conditions as well.

For the rest of you, including those who traverse lakes, especially such bodies of water as the Great Lakes, whose particular weather patterns can, and often do—something I can personally attest to—create challenging conditions to say the least, let's get some weather-savvy information down so you can enjoy your time away from the dock even more.

We all would rather have big puffy fair weather clouds, warm temps, and just the slightest of breezes every time we let go our lines. But it doesn't always work that way and you will be well-served by starting with some really basic and fundamental preparations such as checking your local weather on television, your smart phone app, your desk- or laptop Internet, your boat's VHF weather station channel, or any one of a multitude of other access devices before you get the family out for a day on the water.

As with all of the technical chapters in this book I will avoid any conversation that might cause your eyes to glass over and thus enable you to nod off in a most blissful sleep, as the Bard penned, *"Perchance to dream."*

Instead, I will deal with the basics of what you will need to know. We'll start off the discussion with one of the main factors that can, and will, affect your time out on the water; the wind.

Any conversation about wind must start with the sun. For as long as our star rises and sets—I am told by reliable sources that we have some many billions

▲ Nice weather and a picturesque stopover make for a memorable boating experience. Staying ahead of any possible changes will keep it that way.

▲ Sunrise, and hopefully yet another fine day on the water.

of years to go before it goes super nova—the sun's inevitable dramatic and catastrophic end so, not to worry any time in the near future about things changing too much; of much more concern is global warming but I digress—it is solar energy that causes the wind to blow.

And because Earth's surface heats and cools unevenly—think of the difference between the temperature differences at the equator with those at the poles and everything in between—atmospheric pressure zones are created.

These are the "highs" and "lows" we are most familiar with when listening to our weather reports and it is the air flowing from them—high pressure to low pressure areas—that results in wind. The closer these high and low areas are to each other, the stronger the winds will be. Other factors influencing wind strength and speed is what it is traveling over such as open bodies of water where there is little in the way to slow it down as compared to that presented by a mountain. With this last example, wind can actually increase in speed as it funnels through the "caverns" created by the buildings. I know. I am from New York City, where trying to ascertain the direction of the wind while walking in the streets during a somewhat snotty day can be a bit tricky as well.

Factor in the rotation of the Earth and the direction of the wind will be deflected, known as the Coriolis effect, from side to side; that is, except exactly on the equator.

In the Northern hemisphere this results in winds blowing counterclockwise around low-pressure areas and clockwise around highs, with the opposite holding true for the Southern hemisphere. As well, the direction of the wind is defined as from where it originates. Therefore, a northerly blows from north to south.

One last point to make regarding wind before we move on: The jet stream. A simple definition of jet streams finds them described as fast moving, somewhat narrow and meandering westerly air currents, traveling in the upper atmosphere—if you must know, in that part of Earth's surrounding environment known as the troposphere, some 30,000 to 39,000 feet above sea level where they are known as polar jets. Along with the higher, 33,000 to 52,000 feet above sea level, and not-nearly-as strong subtropical jets, both northern and southern hemispheres have one of each.

They, like all winds on the planet, are powered by the sun's radiation and the Earth's rotation. Jet streams are used by weather forecasters to anticipate varying weather patterns and can be fairly accurate in most cases.

So, unless the Earth stops spinning, we're stuck with the wind. But what about rain?

Weather

Again, as we all learned back in grade school, rain is a major part of the planet's water cycle—remember those ubiquitous posters you made for your sixth grade science fair, illustrating, in various forms of expertise as per your artistic abilities, the concepts of evaporation, condensation, and precipitation? As I recall, my project was not too well received and while I got the facts right, my visuals were a bit off, to say the least. However, my large plastic soda bottle terrarium project lasted a very long time and I was transfixed and amazed when it "rained" inside mine.

Continuing with the conversation, let's mention clouds. Big billows of

▶ A rainy day, even an impending one, is just no fun. And depending on the forecast, it may be wise to cancel your day out.

▲ For time out on the water, it doesn't get any better than this.

puffy cotton and wispy, ethereal and gossamer-like clouds. Ones resembling Everest, K2, and Kilimanjaro dominating the horizon as they drift across the sky. Popcorn looking ones, bunny rabbits and frogs, upside down dragons, babies doing the backstroke, and piled-high ice cream cones.

And yes, those ominous, monstrous-looking, towering dark gray-green ones, their tops sheared off and spitting white-pink-electric-blue lightning from their bases. There are few things in Nature that are more impressive than a big, powerful thunderstorm—that is, from the safety and security of your home and not out at sea. Please, remember that.

Clouds are formed when water, heated by the sun, evaporates from our oceans, lakes, rivers, streams . . . well, you get it, and rises into the air from the Earth's surface. As it gets higher, it begins to cool and the invisible water vapor molecules begin to group together and collect *en masse*. The result is a visible cloud. And should those molecules continue to take up residence in more and more numbers, they become heavy, far too heavy to stay suspended in the air and soon make the return trip to the surface as . . . rain.

That's the short of it and really all I think we need to discuss at this point. However, an important aspect of clouds and cloud formation, and the one we are most concerned with, lies in recognizing what type is overhead or approaching and how it is going to affect your time on the water.

For time immemorial, mariners have looked to the sky in anticipation of planning a voyage or watched carefully as their so far mild passage turned south and became a hellacious storm in a very short time.

Armed with such old saws as, "*Mackerel skies and mares' tails make tall ships take in their sails,*" and this aged ditty, "*When halo rings the moon or sun, rain's approaching on the run,*" as well as everyone's favorite, "*Red sky in morning, sailors take warning. Red sky at night, sailors' delight,*" and while we take for granted all our weather satellites, tables, calculations, advanced science studies and records, selfies and snapshots from the International Space Station, and everything else we have at the ready, there is more than a modicum of folksy truth in these sayings that needs paying attention to.

With mackerel skies, for example, those cirrus clouds, which old salts held looked like they've been scratched at by a chicken, usually escort an approaching warm front, a sure sign of rain and wind.

That halo around the sun or moon is caused by high cirrostratus clouds, composed of ice crystals, and is also indicative of a warm front and rain. And the well-known and celebrated morning and night red sky inference is explained as that beautiful crimson color, caused by the light passing through dust particles, covers the western sky at sunset, where most weather comes from, dry conditions can be expected. However, should those same conditions occur in the morning, this is an indication that the dry air has moved on.

▲ Red sky at night, sailor's delight.

Cirrus clouds.

Cirrocumulus clouds.

Cirrostratus.

As there are many other odes, rhymes, and limericks that concern themselves with bees and other insects, forest animals and birds, comets, coffee grinds, fish, the length of the chin whiskers on a male goat, and just about anything else that has been linked to being a prognosticator of weather, I am sure that if you dig deep enough, you will find the science in the whimsy.

You've seen all of these before so now take a look at the following formations and what they can signify as far as weather prognostication is concerned:

Cirrus clouds—have a thin, slight looking appearance and are a telltale of an approaching warm front.

Cirrocumulus—known as the mackerel sky, while appearing like scales or popcorn, they are actually very small individual clouds, and are indicative of unsettled weather.

Cirrostratus clouds—look as if you can see through the layers and also typify rain.

Cumulus—have a big, white puffy-like appearance and are known as fair weather clouds.

Nimbostratus—a formless, uniformly dark gray layer of clouds that will most likely produce anything from light to a fair amount of rainfall.

Stratocumulus—a lumpy layer of clouds that differ in color from light to dark gray. These can produce some drizzle or on-again-off-again rain and be an indicator of bad weather leaving and clearing on the way.

▲ Cumulus clouds over the ocean.

▲ Nimbostratus. Photo Credit: FreeImages.com/dimitri_c

▲ Cumulonimbus. Photo Credit: FreeImages.com/Brian Mahon

One cloud formation that deserves your undivided attention is the one that grows vertically and extends beyond the troposphere and past twenty thousand feet. These bad boys are known as cumulonimbus; thunder clouds. They can form as individual clouds or as a lineup of towers. When this happens, we have a squall line, which brings with it severe weather, including hail, lightning, tornadoes, as well as rain and, if it's cold enough, snow.

The indisputable fact is that from the moment you become a boat owner, you will be checking both the daily weather report and what is going on in the sky as well as the direction of the wind in your area. Guaranteed. And on that note, please do not ever second-guess the weather. You can always go boating another day.

Fog

And what about fog? Enough said. Do not plan on leaving the dock if you can't see the bow of your boat. It is both disorienting and dangerous and even the most seasoned mariner will choose to stay put until it lifts.

▲ You might be in clear weather with fog lying ahead of you and still quite some distance away. If at all possible, alter your course and either return to your dock or seek a safe berth at a nearby marina. Always use the utmost caution when dealing with this particular weather phenomenon.

At its simplest, it is a very low lying cloud located at the earth's surface, and, of course, right at your dock, that is made up of either water droplets or, if it is just cold enough, ice crystals. Fog usually occurs when the relative humidity, that is the amount of moisture in the air, is at 100 percent.

I am sure you've heard your always-happy and way-too-perky local weather forecaster point out how humid it is and one step outside on a day where it is fairly high is all the confirmation you are going to need. Sticky and uncomfortable and almost feeling as if were thick enough to cut the proverbial knife through, fog, and the ever-present bad hair day it brings, is no fun for boaters. None.

SOME FOGGY FACTS

Phileas Fogg, Jules Verne's protagonist in his 1873 novel *Around The World In Eighty Days,* never did have to deal with the atmospheric condition of his namesake on his Victorian trip that circled the globe. As I've channeled Shakespeare for you boating intellectuals already, you are most likely quite familiar with this quote on his reference to limited visibility in Macbeth: *"Fair is foul, and foul is fair. Hover through the fog and filthy air."* The result of which is murder, mayhem, treachery, and war. Go figure. As well, the father of our country, George Washington, used the cover of a handy local foggy layer to make a clean getaway from lurking British forces during the Battle of Long Island in August of 1776. Lucky for us or we wouldn't have that extended weekend we now enjoy. Tea anyone? On June 6, 1944, the Allied forces used the fog lying across the English Channel to conceal the greatest armada of ships and fighting personnel ever amassed as they landed on the beaches of Normandy, France for the D-Day invasion. It's a toss up for the foggiest places on earth; some say it's Hamilton, New Zealand while others tend to lean towards the Grand Banks off of Newfoundland. Of course some Downeasters might opine that coastal Maine gets the nod. Then there are those snooty Point Reyes, California, habitués who hang their hats on the fact that their location has an average of some two hundred foggy days each year. And let's not forget the dean of American poets, Carl Sandburg's take on the subject: *"The fog comes on little cat feet. It sits looking over harbor and city on silent haunches and then moves on."*

Fog is heavily influenced by several factors including local topography, that being the landscape and geography, wind, and proximity to bodies of water. And while we can extend this conversation and discuss radiation, ground, advection, evaporation, steam, ice, freezing, frontal, hail, pogonip, sea smoke—known as Arctic sea smoke, should you do your family boating in those environs—Garua, usually found near the coasts of Chile and Peru—I don't think too many of you will need to preoccupy yourselves with this location at any time soon—upslope fog, or just plain old "I-can't-see-a-durn-thing kind of fog," as my old friend, and one of the finest old salts I know, Captain Bill Pike laments, it is what it is and should your morning see any kind of reduced visibility that makes you hesitate, even for a brief moment, about going out, I strongly suggest you do not. Instead, get yourself to a local diner and have some breakfast with your family or friends and wait it out. Enough said.

Tides and Currents

Now, completing the holy trinity of weather-related issues is a discussion concerning the rise and fall of the tides and the incoming and outgoing current that comes with them, factors that can and will make docking your boat, no matter how many times you do it, never the same.

I think we've all grown up knowing that the moon, as it travels around the Earth, in its relatively elliptical orbit—a non-circular shape with positions closer, known as perigee, and further away, known as apogee, as it completes its monthly revolution (actually 27.322 days but who's really counting?)—and due to its gravitational attractive force, is the primary cause for the vertical rise and fall of the world's oceans. Allow me a bit of a respite from the conversation here with a slight bit of fanciful diversion on the subject of the moon. This is what often happens to me when I am writing on a subject and another parallel thought creeps in that, once put through the creative process, seems to make sense and becomes germane to the subject under scrutiny.

There is many an old salt whose wakes have crossed mine that because of long-held superstitions—there are few groups more, some would say, irrational, illogical, and unreasonable, on disobeying certain beliefs than mariners—would coordinate their travels, voyages, comings and goings with, among other viewpoints, certain phases of the moon, especially when it is full.

This particular component is nothing to be scoffed at or ignored as the moon not only plays a special role in the natural world but as we all know, and as I am so wont to do yet again, in the words of William Shakespeare, "*There are more things in heaven and earth dear Horatio, than are dreamt of in your philosophy.*"

▲ Throughout history, the moon has occupied a special place in nautical lore.

Since the human species first looked upward at the night sky, the dead orb that accompanies our planet on its own celestial voyage has had a profound effect on humankind.

Such is the upshot on our collective consciousnesses that there's "Moon For The Misbegotten" and "Moon Over Miami"; Native American author William Least Heat Moon; pop star Moon Martin whose 1978 album—yes, in those days it was albums kids, vinyl albums—*Shots From A Cold Nightmare* was received quite well; the infamous Moonies of the 1970s and 80s; H. G. Wells's "From The Earth to The Moon"; moonshine whisky; Pink Floyd's remarkable *Dark Side of The Moon* as well as Van Morrison's mercurial *Moondance*; NFL pro quarterback Warren Moon; other songs such as *Blue Moon*, *(It's only a) Paper Moon*, *By The Light of The Silvery Moon*, *Shine on Harvest Moon*, the Rolling Stones' *Moonlight Mile*, and Warren Zevon's *They Moved the Moon*; Streit's Moon Strips matzohs; of course there's always howling at the moon and the Moonwalk, made famous by pseudo-human Michael Jackson.

Then there is the well-known Man in The Moon, not to be confused by the movie of almost-the-same-name, *The Man on The Moon,* nor the movie of the same name starring Jim Carey as hell-bent-for-destruction comedian Andy Kaufman; moon pies (they came in artificial chocolate and strawberry flavored); Moon Dog, the Viking-clad existential poet who, until he died, made it his life's work to stand on a street corner in New York City; and then there was his parallel universe buddy, Moondoggie, the half-wit surfer dude from those Frankie Avalon and Annette Funicello flicks.

For those of us who grew up on the absolutely astonishing Goodnight Moon children's book, it is still a source of wonder and, while sitting 180 degrees from the sublime is the persistent and absurd sophomoric inclination toward mooning—just where this came from is a mystery that deserves to stay that way; the famous comic strip of the 1940s and 50s, Moon Mullins; Frank Moon, who played the role of the doctor on the hit television show, The A-Team; D. H. Lawrence's, *"the new moon, of no importance"*; lots of Asian kids having Moon as a surname; many references in literature, poetry, and music to moon-faced girls, none of which I can name right now but I know they exist; Moon Unit Zappa, daughter of Frank Zappa, transcendental leader and driving force of the 1960s band, The Mothers of Invention; the movie *Moonstruck* with Cher and Nicholas Cage; a moon reference from Coleridge's "The Rime of the Ancient Mariner" reads thus: *"The moving Moon went up the sky. And nowhere did abide; Softly she was going up, And a star or two beside"*; to classic 1950s Honeymooner Jackie Gleason's exasperated signature shout as Brooklyn, New York, bus driver/Everyman Ralph Cramden, "To the moon Alice!"

Of course, we are all familiar with the nursery rhyme line where the cow jumped over the moon, and, by the way, ran away with the spoon; the moon adventures of Baron von Munchausen; and who could ever forget the cheesy 1950s black and white sci-fi film classic, *Cat-Women of the Moon*. Not me, that's for sure.

In colonial America, the month of March was the time of the Fish Moon; for the Chinese, it was known as the Sleepy Moon; the Cherokee tribe called it the Windy Moon while the Choctaw and Dakota Sioux knew it as The Big Famine Moon and the Moon When Eyes Are Sore From Bright Snow, respectively.

For those ancient and rascally Celts it was the Moon Of Winds; Medieval Englanders christened it the Chaste Moon while the Neo Pagans naturally dubbed it the Death Moon—go figure, Pagans. And to those people inhabiting New Guinea, the appellation for the full moon occurring in March ranged from Rainbow Fish to Palalo Worm to Open Sea to Rain and Wind Moon. A rose by any other name, eh?

Then there's the whole tide thing coupled with our own bodily makeup consisting of lots of water—while actual amounts vary, it centers around 60 percent in adults—and the fact that we begin life by swimming around in amniotic fluid for nine months and the possible effect the moon could have on that. I could easily go on and on and fill several more pages but I think you catch my drift. So, bottom line here? Superstitions set aside, don't discount the effect that the moon has on us mere mortals.

Let us continue. While the sun does bring some influence to bear, its distance, some 93 million miles from Earth compared with the mere 239,125-mile as-the-crow-flies—while there are several derivations of this saying, it remains an idiomatic expression defining the shortest distance between two points—stretch away of our moon, enables our nearest celestial body to have a bit more sway.

To wit, if you've never been to the Bay of Fundy between Canada's New Brunswick and Nova Scotia, where the tidal drop can top 50-plus feet, the world's most dramatic change, you haven't seen how drastic this natural phenomenon can be.

In fact, the tides are responsible for much more than just affecting how much line you will need to tie your boat up to a non-floating dock. For coastal locations, for example, the tides are quite important and vital to what marine biologists call intertidal ecology and among other subjects, the study is concerned with the organisms that exist between the high, when they are underwater, and low tide, exposed to the air, regions. Besides these organisms being essential for establishing the proper ecosystem balance between predation and prey—eat or be eaten—in some tropical and subtropical areas, a far more important situation exists.

▲ Always be aware of water depth especially in areas not clearly marked. While this may appear to be okay, when the tide runs out, you may find yourself high and dry for the next six or so hours.

▲ As you can clearly see, this is the same area at low tide. Take heed if the birds are walking.

Mangrove trees, because of their ability to exist in salt and brackish coastal waters where the tidal rise and fall cover and expose their root systems, are a critical and important component of the ecological health of these areas. However, once the trees have established their habitats, the substantial roots provide surroundings for oyster beds and slow down the water system. This last ability can serve to protect these coastal areas from erosion during storm surges. But the most important is the rather unique ecosystem that these trees provide as they establish habitats for algae, sponges, shrimps, and crabs among a host of others in which to thrive and thus, continue to feed the many species that, in the grand scheme of things, inhabit our oceans. Circle of life.

As stated, tide is the vertical rise, known as incoming/flood, and fall, called the outgoing/ebb of water with current being the horizontal movement associated with the tidal change. And as it can vary from location to location as the tides rise and fall, as well as how fast the current is moving, knowing when each is occurring is a key component in such tasks as anchoring, maintaining your course, and especially in docking maneuvers.

While it follows the Earth through the cosmos, the moon's monthly cycles see it going through four stages, or more familiarly, phases. As pictured here, the first is known as a new moon with the first quarter, full, and last quarter, also known as the third quarter, following.

New and full moons result when the sun and the Earth and its ever-present satellite are as directly in line with one another as can be. When this celestial event takes place—called a syzygy for all you Scrabble players—the high and low tides, due to the sun adding to the increase of the moon's gravitational influence, become higher and lower than usual. These tides are known as spring tides and as you will discover, have nothing to do with that particular season of the year. Of more concern is that the current, due to the increase in the tidal rise and fall, is stronger at these times and can add, and depending on your location, to take all this into consideration while involved in docking maneuvers. Throw a bit of wind into the mix, and these kinds of situations will definitely test your skills, mettle, and patience.

As Nature is always in balance and hates chaos, there is the flip side of spring tides, a less extreme tidal sequence known as neap tides, that comes into play during the moon's first and last quarter phases. For all you etymologists out there—a word origin expert—neap comes from an Anglo Saxon expression meaning "without the power." Kind of fits when you think of it.

In this case, the sun, Earth, and moon, with the latter in its first and third quarter stages, finds the trio separated by 90 degrees when viewed from Earth. When this occurs, and because the sun is partially blocking the moon's gravitational influence, the tidal range will be at its minimum.

The movement created by tides is also being considered as alternative energy sources. Tidal stream generators, designed to harness the ebb and flow, have already been put into use in the Bay of Fundy, South Korea, France, Canada, Russia, China, and the UK with plants scheduled to be built in the Philippines and India. I find it kind of unsettling how the U.S. seems to always be behind with this kind of forward thinking and technology. Can you say oil lobby?

Tides occur four times a day, and depending on your geographical location, at about every six hours. Spring and neap tides are separated by an average of seven days and the time between high and low tides is known as slack, when there is little movement in the water, and can also vary in its duration depending on where you boat or travel.

A Simple Explanation

Samantha Kreisler, at age five, figured out what causes the waves at the beach: *"All the whales out in the ocean turn around and move their tales up and down. Yep, that's how it happens, Dad."*

When setting out for the day, as with checking the weather forecast, it's a good practice to also know when the high and low tide is. Your local marina will usually have it posted or you can bring it up on your GPS/chartplotter screen. And of course, have that weather App you so wisely loaded on your smart phone at the ready as well.

In addition, and because I am a devotee of having redundancy aboard— extra oil, oil and fuel filters, belts, and a whole bunch of other stuff I cover in the BASIC MAINTENANCE chapter—you need to have the latest copy of your area's tidal book in your onboard library and right next to your ship's log.

On the east coast, we have the *Eldridge Tide and Pilot Book* as the essential resource for tides and currents that cover the ports from Nova Scotia to Key West.

It is chock full of information on GPS and electronic navigation, marine weather, Federal regulations, navigation rules, coastal piloting tips, and emergency first aid.

In addition, there are tidal reference books and apps for other parts of the country including the Gulf Coast, Alaska, the Pacific Northwest, and the rest of the western coast of the US.

The only advice I can leave you with is to take heed of the weather. While you can control most of what goes on with your boat, its mechanics and daily operation, weather is the one thing you cannot manage, restrain, run, sway, or have any influence over. I have been caught in one too many a hellacious situation—yes, one is one too many—and it is nothing one goes out to meet. Bad weather is to be avoided at all costs.

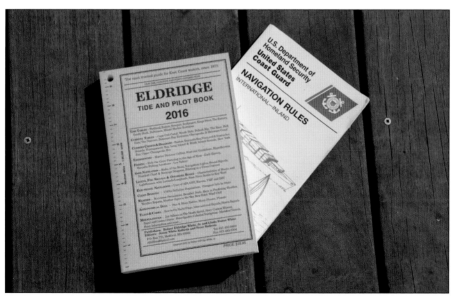

▲ Both this local Eldridge and the latest edition of the USCG's Rules of the Road are indispensable reference books to have on board at all times.

Thunder and Lightning

While many stories filled our young minds as children, this spectacular phenomenon of nature is not, as in the Rip Van Winkle tale, the ghosts of Hendrick "Henry" Hudson's crew playing nine-pins, nor is it Thor's mighty hammer, an angry Zeus, the Hindu God Indra, Set of Egyptian mythology fame, Oya, the pesky goddess and consort of Shango of the Sub-Saharan Yoruba religion, the Australian Mamaragan from Aboriginal folklore, the Iroquois and Huron native indigenous tribal peoples' Thunderbird, or China's Thirty-six Gods of Thunder, just to mention a few.

Lightning and thunder are the ultimate conjoined twins and dealing with them can often be a bit dicey and downright dangerous.

When that rumble comes, what you are hearing is the explosion of an electrical charge sending out not only the flash of light but the sound of all that released energy. It has to do with the sudden increase in air temperature and pressure and the resultant rapid expansion of the atmosphere around the bolt.

You can calculate how far the distance is from the strike to your location by counting the seconds between seeing the initial visual flash and the first clap,

▲ A lightning strike, while inherently beautiful, can be dangerous. Photo Credit: FreeImages.com/Danny du Bruyne.

crack, peal, or rumble of thunder. The rule of thumb—that most stretchable of principles, adhering to the ideology of non-adherence to any accurate or reliable source and instead is all about almost, roughly, nearly, more or less . . . well, you get it—is about one mile for every five seconds.

It is highly unlikely that any new boat will not have an American Boat & Yacht Council (ABYC) approved bonding system installed for lightning protection. For those of you interested in a brokerage boat, make sure you check with your salesperson to make certain the boat is properly bonded. If not, and you are keen on buying it, arrange for a licensed marine electrician to do the work as per ABYC standards. Could be a good bargaining chip in your negotiations.

What this does is tie all the major metals aboard your boat, thus enabling any possible lightning strike, much like a lightning rod does on land, to go to ground; in this case, into the water.

The concept of this kind of protection is known as Faraday's Cage, named after Michael Faraday, the nineteenth century scientist who first put forth this principle, and provides a cone of protection around your boat. A lightning bolt can reach up to five miles in length, raise the temperature of the surrounding air to as high as 50,000° F, and can contain some 100 million volts. Not to be messed with. And although all those statistics on the chances of being hit by lightning—or bitten by a shark—are fairly high, who wants to be the one? Not me. I'd rather try hitting the Mega Ball Lottery. Sooner or later, someone gets the right numbers. Back to reality: in order to drive this home, here are two clear-cut and well-defined rules that every mariner must adhere to.

RULE #1

Do not ever leave the dock, nor even think, consider, mull or muse, contemplate, plan or ponder, or any combination thereof about letting your lines go, if there is even a chance, possibility, risk, probability, likelihood, hint, or any combination thereof of a thunderstorm coming your way.

RULE #2: SEE RULE #1.

Levity aside shipmates, this kind of weather is not to be trifled with. Thunderstorms, and the resultant possibility of dangerous wind, driving rain, huge seas, and lightning are life threatening and are, I repeat, to be avoided at all costs.

Again, I speak from experience. Having been caught on the outer fringes of Hurricane Hugo in September of 1989 north of Charleston, South Carolina, been landside in the throes of Superstorm Sandy on the New Jersey shore in 2012, as well as finding myself jammed up in dealing with several squalls throughout the years is quite enough for a lifetime and has instilled in me much more than a healthy respect for what can happen away from the dock. When it comes to dicey weather, stay safe.

A NAUTICAL ASIDE

Here's Capt. Ed Baker's, my dear friend, co-conspirator-in-arms, and one of the best skippers around take on being on the water: *"I'll take buoyancy over gravity any day. You go down in a plane you're more or less toast. You're in the water and you have a fairly good chance of getting yourself back to land. That's all I have to say on the matter."*

www.skyhorsepublishing.com

8. Rules of The Road, Lights, Day Shapes, the Buoy System & Basic Seamanship

"The mind of the master of a vessel is rooted deep in the timbers of her, though he command for a day or a decade . . ."

—Stephen Crane, Author

*W*hile being in the hunt for a boat, you've most likely picked up a few of the more common sayings that are here and there:

- *Give someone a fish and they will eat for a day. Teach them how to fish and they will sit in a boat and drink beer all day.*
- *All sailors and fishermen are liars except you and me. And I'm not so sure about you.*
- *Don't forget to check the drain plug.*

And of course, the one that will get us into the conversation of this chapter:

- *Red right returning.*

Just as there are rules of the road for driving a car, so too there is a system in place that everyone who leaves the dock, and gets back, needs to be aware of and follow to the letter. Of course there are those who for a variety of all the wrong reasons, which I cannot, even after all these many years, figure out just why, do not adhere to even the most basic of commonsense regulations.

Let's open up the conversation a bit here with an opinion. Mine. Again, following the logic of licensing all those who wish to operate a car or other like machinery. Boaters should also be required to, at the very least, show some

▲ Always follow the prescribed channel markers when entering or leaving. The safe way is clearly indicated and you run the risk of getting yourself into some trouble should you stray off the marks.

www.skyhorsepublishing.com

▲ No matter where you boat, having a clear understanding of the basic rules of safe navigation will help make your day, as well as that of everyone else out on the water, that much more enjoyable.

understanding of the basic navigation rules. Indeed, there are some states that require, among registration, for boat owners to take a safe boating course in order to be in compliance. I agree.

And while there are some old salts, with whom I have gotten into spirited arguments, who say if you have been around long enough, you should have no trouble at all with acting in accordance with commonsense, my response is, so what's the problem?

I say this because as boating increases in popularity and entry-level access becomes increasingly attractive and affordable, there will be more and more boaters taking to the bays, rivers, and coastal communities. For this reason alone, the need for education and situational awareness is important.

Some of the larger dealerships, such as MarineMax, have teamed up with local Coast Guard Auxiliary officers to host annual safe-boating courses.

The programs are designed to familiarize a novice or intermediate boater with boat handling and safety. It also can be a refresher course for more experienced boaters.

"This informative, hands-on course is a seminar version of the USCG Auxiliary's popular online course," MarineMax Panama City Beach, Florida, sales consultant and broker Bob Fowler said in a statement. "We try to have fun while interacting with personal instructors by sharing important safety practices, operational skills and maintenance advice that will keep you and your family protected while on the water."

Topics to be covered include general boating basics and knowledge; restrictions and regulations; required and recommended safety equipment; how to safely operate and navigate a boat; and how to handle problems.

Other subjects can include trailering, storing and protecting a boat, and how to properly operate when fishing, waterskiing, or boating on a river.

There are usually fees associated with these kinds of programs but you will have to inquire about that as you seek them out with the particular dealership or sponsor that may be involved. Other excellent resources to use for this kind of information are Discover Boating (www.discoverboating.com) and BoatUS (www.boatus.com) as well as are the USCG Auxiliary and the US Power Squadron for your area. If you are going to invest your time and money in boating, it pays to make sure you and your family have the best and safest experience possible.

With that said, let's move on to just what those rules are. To begin with, you should have a copy of, and be familiar with, the aforementioned *International-Inland USCG Navigation Rules.*

Available at most marine retail stores and marinas, this indispensable book is a great reference tool, having all the information, including clear-cut pictures and representations along with lights, sounds and signals, and shapes, for understanding the various situations that can and will occur while underway and the safe, practical, and preferred method for dealing with them. While there are separate rules for operating in international and inland waters, and many are similar and overlap, for all useful purposes our discussion will deal with the latter.

Basically, the inland rules cover all vessels navigating upon U.S. inland waters as well as those U.S. vessels entering the Canadian waters of the Great Lakes as long as there is no conflict with the laws of that country. Vessels are described as "every description of water craft, including non-displacement craft and seaplanes, used or capable of being used as a means of transportation on the water." It's a broad definition but one that covers all the bases.

The rules go on to explain the necessity and accountability of complying with the regulations as well as laying out, in detail, just what they are. And while the specificity of those designed in both word and action to prevent and eliminate the chances of any kind of collision, it is within the wording of Rule 2, Responsibility of the General Inland Rules, commonly known around the docks as the Rule of Good Seamanship, #2(a), and the General Prudential Rule, #2(b), that I find the one that can often make the most difference in assisting you in taking the right course of action when faced with certain situations. The following is right from the book, word for word:

> Rule 2(a): Nothing in these rules shall exonerate any vessel, or the owner, master, or crew thereof, from the consequences or any neglect to comply with these Rules or of the neglect of any precaution when may be required by the ordinary practice of seamen, of by the special circumstances of the case.

> Rule 2(b): In construing and complying with these Rules due regard shall be had to all dangers of navigation and collision and to any special circumstances, including the limitations of the vessels involved, which may make a departure from these Rules necessary to avoid immediate danger.

Simply put, if you need to take the kind of action that will avoid any chance or possibility of a collision, and even if that action is in violation of a particular rule, do it. Of course, thinking ahead and realizing that not everyone either knows the rules or adheres to them should enable you, while you are enjoying your boating time, to keep a sharp eye out into the seaway for any action you may need to take well in advance. Don't ever second-guess that the other boater knows what they are doing. It's as if you were playing chess and planning five moves ahead.

For example, Rule 14 states that when two power driven vessels are approaching each other head on, each shall alter their course to starboard and pass port to port. However, what if the other boat is not complying, or in doing so and because of circumstances around them, may be finding that particular maneuver difficult to make happen?

It is now up to you to perhaps slow down, assess the situation to make sure that any deviation on your part will not become a problem for any other vessel and instead, take proper action that may not have you passing port to port of the other vessel. This is an extremely important concept and one that you need to take with you each and every time you are out on the water.

Here's another familiar scenario you will most assuredly come up against. Should you be faced with a crossing situation, and if the other boat is on your starboard side, you are considered the give-way vessel and must alter your course so as not to cross that boat's bow and instead, pass safely astern. However, should the opposite be the case, and the boat is approaching to cross you from your port side, you are now the stand-on vessel and have the right of way. But take care in these situations. Should that other boat be a sailing vessel, and one only under sail—but if under motor power or under power with its sails up, it is to be considered a power driven vessel and is now governed by those rules—it has the right of way and regardless of which side it is approaching from, you are required to pass well astern. In addition, if the crossing vessel is a large boat or a commercial tug and tow or any other kind that may be unable to comply because of its present activity, size, position, or any other factor where you are better able to navigate, you should always pass astern or give it as wide a berth as possible.

In overtaking situation, you are always the give-way vessel and must either contact the boat in front of you via your VHF and on the working channel for your area, for permission to pass on either the port or starboard side or use prescribed whistle or horn signals.

On those whistle or horn signals, there is also an approved regimen when using these audible sounds. Let's take our example of those two vessels approaching each other. Not only are they required to alter to starboard and pass port to port but will also indicate their intentions by giving one short blast on the boat's horn. You are not to take any further action until the stand-on vessel acknowledges it is safe to do so with a corresponding signal. If you are on the VHF and speaking with the other vessel, the usual conversation goes something like this:

"*Northbound approaching vessel passing Pirate's Point, this is* Vagabond. *I would like to see you on one.*"

"*Right* Vagabond, *this is* Petrel. *One it is.*"

"Petrel, Vagabond. *Understood. One whistle.*"

In this way, each vessel knows and understands what the other is preparing to do. Here's a brief rundown on those horn signals:

ONE SHORT BLAST

approaching head on and altering course to pass port to port and when overtaking a vessel on its starboard side, your port side.

TWO SHORT BLASTS

approaching head on and altering course to pass starboard to starboard and when overtaking a vessel on it port side, your starboard side.

Other horn signals include one short blast when leaving the dock and all lines are off. Should you be backing down, add another three blasts to indicate your engine(s) are in reverse. Please make sure, before any maneuvers are done, that the way is clear without any boat traffic coming from any direction that may put you and the approaching vessel, or any others, in a compromising situation. When in doubt, and if a dangerous situation is starting to shape up, you should not hesitate to give five short blasts on the horn as an indication that something untoward could be developing.

And think of this before you try any move that again, just might put you or the other boat in a compromising situation: It's what I term the WHAT IF factor. What if your engine fails? What if you pick up a plastic bag in your raw water intake? What if you hit a submerged object? What if some knucklehead throws you a big wake because he passed by too close? (Please remember, you are responsible for your wake; take heed of no-wake zones and be courteous when passing another boat, paddle boarder, canoeist, or kayaker. Give them lots of room or slow down to a safe idle speed.) In other words, never assume that you can clear that oncoming vessel or overtake another boat so, for example, you can get into the channel before they do. Take your time, enjoy the day, and when at the wheel of your boat, always do the right thing and do it well in advance. Don't be that "other boater."

Getting back to our Rules of The Road, and as I previously mentioned sail boats, let's cover some points regarding having to deal with them. Yes, when under sail, and with any inboard engine or outboard motor off, the vessel is considered a sailboat and therefore, has the right of way.

My advice? You see a sailboat, stay clear. Slow down. Turn around. Change course if it is safe. I will not weigh in on the gulf that exists between powerboaters and sailboaters—"stink pots" and "blow boats" or "ragbaggers" respectively—as each have their own mindset, attitude, and right to be on the water.

▲ With sails up and engine off, sailboats should always be given the right of way.

However, in busy harbors, or in tight and close quarters situations, it's best to stay ahead of the curve here and always take prudent action in terms of safety and collision avoidance. And, again, should that sailboat have its sails up and its motor on, it is now considered a power driven vessel and is governed by the same rules as you adhere to. In all cases, whether with sailboats or other powerboats, early and substantial action should become part of your nautical sense. Make any course changes obvious. Don't wait. Don't hesitate.

As far as the required navigation lights, your boat will be equipped with everything you need as per your vessel's length; red to port, green to starboard and any mast or stern lights as required.

In addition, every other boat out on the water will need to display certain lights at night that will indicate size and in many cases, what it is involved in. For example, tugboats either pushing from behind or alongside, or towing barges, will have a certain array of lights to indicate such a situation. In addition, fishing vessels, composite vessels, commercial boats on rivers and lakes, as well as others will all have specific lights that must be displayed. As well there are certain day shapes, cones and rounds for example, that you should become familiar with as these are indicators that certain activities are taking place so that you can take appropriate action. Case in point are a pair

▲ Navigation lights are critical for safe boating operation during limited visibility and at night. The latest technology, such as these NaviLED PRO series from Hella Marine (www.hellamarine.com) offers greater illumination with a drastic reduction in power draw. Photo Credit: Hella Marine

▲ One of the special day shapes, in this case a black ball indicating a vessel is at anchor, can be readily seen in the rigging of this Coast Guard boat.

of black cones, placed point to point in the rigging of a vessel indicates it is fishing by trawling, that is dragging a net astern as you should be aware of this in case your present course may have you crossing it.

When you enroll in your safe boating course, again strongly suggested and just about as mandatory for new boaters as anything else I can think of, you will get a comprehensive review of all the Rules, signals, lights, day shapes, aids to navigation, and so much more than what we have touched on here and can be included in this edition. As well, there are many other resources you can tap for this information including your own on-board copy of the Navigation Rules (www.prostarpublications.com), along with a wide variety of extremely useful plastic placards (www.sentinelpressllc.com), which can be kept in a handy binder and at the ready should you need to refer to it, and which are also available at your marina store. BoatUS (www.boatus.org/guide) offers a terrific online boating safety guide that is as good as it gets and is one I highly recommend.

Aids to Navigation

Just as there are highways, roads, interstates, turnpikes, and the like for our land-based transportation needs, so too are there designated channels and seaways for you to always pay attention to while out on the water.

▲ While they come in many shapes, sizes, and colors, knowing what buoys and other markers stand for is an important part of spending your time on the water.

Indicated by a series of buoys and markers, the clear and preferred way or channel while leaving or coming back, is your sign that this is the safe route to travel. It is the correct depth, is free of obstacles, hazards, or dangers, and will eventually get you where you are going. Easy to read visually, and along with checking your progress on the information presented on your GPS/chartplotter screen, navigating any channel should present little difficulty even for the novice boater. And as we've discussed here before, getting familiar with local knowledge is quite helpful and asking your marina manager or dockmates, even making arrangements to follow another boat out and back for the first time, will get you invaluable information and experience to use as you get more familiar and comfortable with your area when out on the water.

Leaving your dock, the green markers, if numbered will be odd, and are on your port. The red ones, if numbered will be even, and to starboard. Coming back in, as in the all-to-familiar "red right returning" catchphrase, it will be the opposite.

Buoys can be lit or unlit, fitted with sound producing devices such as horns or bells, and be of several shapes and functions such as mid-channel markers, preferred channels, junctions, obstructions, or security zones among others. While the USCG has jurisdiction over federal waters, privately maintained

▲ Your GPS/Chartplotter screen has all the information on every aid to navigation in the area you will be traveling through.

buoys can be maintained by local, state, and private agencies. Always check with your local marina for any channels or markers you should know about.

A good reference tool to have is the free download of US Chart #1, with over 100 pages of important chart symbols and other information that will be of help whenever you are underway and reading your GPS. (www.nauticalcharts.noaa. gov/mcd/chartno1.htm). In addition, as with most informational data, there are some great video presentations on YouTube and other sites that cover this topic in every detail.

Basic Seamanship

I clearly remember one particular time I was taking a boat south to Ft. Lauderdale, Florida, and upon arrival—it was late in the evening, obviously dark, and with a rip-roaring flood tide running as well—was told to proceed to a certain dock and look for the only open space between two rather large megayachts. I was told their names over the VHF and yes indeed, I agreed, they were very large.

My charge was a mere 90 feet in length, with no bow or stern thrusters, and when we arrived at the location I judged I had about 120 feet or so to work with.

"Okay boys," I said to my two deckhands, "We're going to have one shot at this. Hang all the fenders port side to. Get that forward line on real fast, snug it up even faster and I'll swing the stern in. Got it?"

Nothing was said as they quickly disappeared from the wheelhouse. As a crew, we had been in tight situations before and each of us knew exactly what the others were going to do before it was done.

End of story, I slid my boat right into that spot as I proudly watched my crew secure the lines with aplomb and expertise, as the entire ship's complement from the yacht on my bow to the one astern looked on. We got a round of applause and no one saw, or heard, my knees knocking.

For those of us who partake in this watery life, very few things are as impressive as a crew that just knows how to handle a boat. It is an on-going process that is constantly changing and I have found out, even after all these years, no two dockings are ever the same. Wind, current, whatever, can all play havoc with your approach, setup, and line handling.

One of the suggestions I discuss with first timers and novice boaters alike is to try and think as if you were playing chess. And what if you don't play chess? It doesn't matter. My intention here is to get you to think three, four, even five moves ahead.

Your new boat tutorial and instructional time will be well spent and do not be too concerned with your initial experience. This is the kind of stuff that can only be understood, practiced, and finally mastered with hands on the wheel time. Given the time, you too will gain the kind of confidence that will have you walking down the dock with a bit of a salty swagger in your step. And remember, slow goes the pro.

First, you need to have a clear understanding of how your particular boat deals with the water, and especially when you are docking or in close quarters situations.

If you go with any of the joystick-controlled engines, or those equipped with pod drives, you definitely already have a leg up. Giving you the most control, even with wind and current, your learning curve and comfort level will be reached a lot sooner than with traditional equipment.

I am sure you have the basics. Moving forward, port is to the left and starboard is to the right. Should you be looking aft, it does not change. With forward propulsion, turn the wheel to port, and your boat will go that way. To starboard, and it will turn to the right. Easy? Of course it is. Like riding a bike. Now try that in reverse. Hold that thought for a moment.

Props turn either left or right when put into forward gear and therefore, are called left or right handed. Now, with outboard and pod or I/O equipped boats, the engine—for the former—and the lower units—for the latters—are the rudders. With an inboard engine, the prop's thrust is run past an actual rudder that acts as the steering mechanism.

For your outboard, and for that matter, on any boat, it's always prudent and wise to approach the dock slowly and with a game plan taking into consideration the wind and current. Your instructional period will be most helpful in honing your instincts and getting to know how your boat reacts under different conditions. This is a key concept in getting the handling knack around the dock.

With coming alongside on the port side, once you are in the correct position, and for most that would be about a half boat's length away, with forward propulsion and your rudder/engine amidships, it's time to put your wheel over to starboard to move your bow out. Slip your engine into gear for a quick moment and place it back into neutral, this causing your stern to move to port and your bow out and away. To put the final touch on things, turn your wheel all the way to port and your engine(s) in reverse. This will slide you right into the dock where you can get a line on a cleat.

Okay. As I don't want to overwhelm you with everything you may need to know at this point—telling is a lot different than doing and you will get it, and much more, as soon as you get behind the wheel of your new boat with your instructor—but putting your engine in reverse, with a right handed prop, rudder amidships, and an inboard engine, will usually swing the stern to port.

Getting all this under your belt, and becoming almost automatic when setting up any kind of docking maneuver is just a matter of practice. We can spend pages and pages here with pictures, drawings, arrows and the like and it would have no real impact unless you were actually doing it. In order for you to visualize what happens, check out the many offerings on YouTube, BoatUS, U.S. Power Squadrons, or any of the other on-line offerings that are under the heading of "how to dock a boat" in the search window.

Anchoring

Okay, so you've gotten away from the dock without any incident, and while your hands are still glued tightly to the wheel, and your neck is craning around like a sea gull eyeing someone's sandwich lying there on the beach, you've found the proper channel.

As you've now managed to relax some, and after checking the GPS, notice that your destination, a wonderful, quiet and picturesque anchorage for that special family lunch you have planned, is but a mere half hour away. Not bad skipper. Not bad.

You arrive, power down to idle, look around and notice everyone is now looking at you. It's time to anchor or, in the salty vernacular, throw the hook.

Your new boat will be equipped with the suitable anchoring apparatus as per its size. And grabbing some proper bottom, and holding it, is not all that difficult. I am sure your tutorial session included how to accomplish this but let's go over some of the basic techniques.

▲ Proper anchoring involves letting out the right amount of scope and allowing for tidal swing. Photo Credit: FreeImages.com/Joe Zlomek

Your anchor, and while there are many types for various uses, with the most popular being the fluke or Danforth type, is designed to dig into the bottom and hold your boat in place. Since no one anchor is good for every use, and if you plan on boating in a specific area, you might want to check into what is preferred for that particular application. Or, if you have travel in your future, carry a spare. Check with your boat builder on their recommendations.

In order for it to work properly, there are some factors that you should know about. The line attaching the end of the anchor to your boat is known as the rode. This in turn, might have a length of chain attached to it that is shackled to the anchor itself and then to the line. In some cases, the rode is a complete length of chain as this not only helps the anchor reach the bottom quicker but also tends to be a bit stronger in swift currents.

Check your GPS chartplotter for the proper depth and bottom conditions. Obviously a flat surface area is preferred. Once you have your spot picked out, you will drop you anchor with enough rode to equal about seven times the depth. Most likely you have an automatic windlass aboard, a handy piece of equipment that will lower and pick up your anchor, automatically stowing your rode in the anchor locker as it brings it in.

▲ While this Danforth-type anchor is destined for use on a large yacht, the style is the same for smaller vessels.

▲ This boat is equipped with a plow-type anchor. With outstanding holding power in grass, mud, and sand, and good in resetting themselves in windy and strong current conditions, they can be found on sailboats and larger vessels.

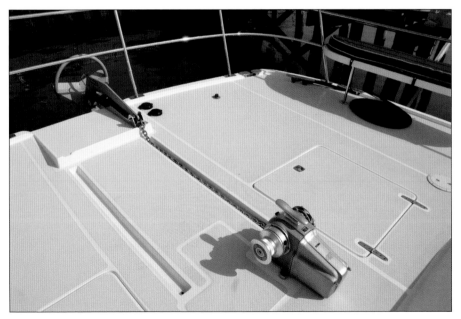

▲ The anchor windlass on the bow of this power catamaran has a channel to hold the chain rode as well as a pair of deck-mounted foot switches forward for up and down operations.

And as it is a rather simple operation, familiarity with the windlass is accomplished with some practice. Turn on the breaker, release the safety anchor chock, and either depress the deck button forward—down or up—or if so equipped, at the helm controls.

If you are in a tidal area, check at which point it is at and if running out or flooding. This will determine how you position your boat. And always consider swing room as this will change with the tide.

So, with the water at, for example, ten feet deep, you are going to need about seventy feet of rode to make your anchoring successful. With all chain rode, it's about five to one. This length is known as scope. Put your bow into the direction of where the current is coming from, or if in a non-tidal area, into the wind if any, and let your anchor drop until it hits the bottom. After letting out about 1/3 of the rode, cinch it up to the proper bow cleat and watch as your boat swings around and you feel the anchor dig in. You can now let out the rest of the rode and once cleated off again, give the engine a quick bump in reverse. That should do it. Enjoy the afternoon, and keep an eye on shore points to make sure your anchor has not pulled out.

When you are ready to leave, put your engine in forward gear at idle speed, and as you do, get your line or chain coming in until you are directly over the anchor. A bit more forward will break it out of the bottom after which you can get it up and secured in place. If you are not able to wash your deck area clean, make sure you do so when you get back to the dock.

Again, as with a lot of this instructional information, there is loads of great video footage showing many anchoring situations that you may have to deal with. In your search window, type in "how to anchor a boat" and you will have your pick of exactly what you are looking for.

Tying Up Your Boat

If you are getting a dock space in a marina, you will need the proper dock lines and fenders. It's a simple matter and one that your marina manager can assist you with.

Depending on which side you will be docking on, either port side to or starboard, you should have enough fenders on that side to protect your boat and keep it off the side of the dock.

A bow line forward and a stern line aft, along with forward and aft spring lines amidships should do the trick.

Proper cleating off is done by first taking a turn around the cleat then taking the line around each horn once before locking it in with a half hitch over one of the horns. In this way your boat will sit nicely in its slip, properly tied and fended off.

▲ With the right lines and protection, your boat will be safe and secure.

▲ Begin by taking your dock line around the base of the cleat.

▲ Next take a turn around the cleat.

▲ A figure eight around the cleat horns comes next.

Rules of The Road, Lights, Day Shapes, the Buoy System & Basic Seamanship • **145**

▲ Finally, lock the line in.

Welcome. You have arrived.

9. Safety

"A ship in harbor is safe, but that is not what ships are built for."
— John A. Shedd, American Writer and Scholar

*N*ow hear this. This chapter is the most important one in the book.

"You better know what to do when something goes south out there because you can't get out and change a flat tire," a crusty, wise, and knowledgeable old salt once said to me way back when I first set my course on this nautical life.

That was more than sage advice and I have kept his counsel to heart over all these years, and I make the safety factor of boating a number-one priority.

I remember one day out on the water that, while enjoying clear skies and light winds, saw me thinking on my feet with the possibility of facing a balky starter motor.

While those aboard were busy with the steady action during some drift fishing, I noted a rather annoying sound coming from below decks during the last start up, and decided to have a look.

Sounds are important aboard a boat and once you get to know how everything on yours is supposed to resonate to your ears, you will know, I promise you, when something is amiss.

Of course, once there and looking here and there, no display sign came bouncing out of the engine, a brightly colored cartoon-like card happily bobbing up and down like a jack-in-the-box on the end of a spring, exclaiming HERE IT IS, with a finger symbol pointing to the exact spot of the trouble.

My careful examination, starting first with all the wiring, finally turned up a very hot outer casing on the started motor. How hot? Well, I figured, at the lightning-fast rate I pulled my palm away after laying a hand on, it could have very well fried an egg. I prefer over medium please. That's how hot.

Anyway, with the culprit identified, I figured I had at least one shot at getting my engine turned over. Being a diesel, that's all I had to do and once fired up, it would run all day as long as I didn't shut it down. But what to do now?

I sat back in the engine compartment for several moments and ran through a number of scenarios. Wrapping an ice pack around it came to mind just before a rather, if I do say so myself, unique eureka flash—not the town in northwest California or the one in Oregon or even the one in Arkansas—but an aha-bingo-wow-I-got-it moment!

Knowing I had a CO_2 extinguisher aboard, I quickly fetched it and, making sure I had plenty of proper ventilation space, began blowing a coating of very cold gas at the starter motor, which instantly began to envelop the casing in a soft white cocoon—a salty interpretation, to my eyes right then and there, of a below decks nautical Currier & Ives-like painting, and, presenting, just perhaps, a solution to my current dilemma.

Bounding up to the deck and then up to the bridge, I hit the starter button and heard not the stomach churning click-click-click of a faulty starter motor but instead the resolute and confident turning over of my diesel engine.

We had a great rest of the day, with a good catch and an equally good time bolstered by the constant and sure sound of my reliable six-cylinder powerplant.

When I got back to the dock, I pulled off the errant part and sent it out for repair the next day while ordering a brand new one at the same time. The learned counsel of my wise mentor was front and center in my mind.

To the point, I strongly recommend taking a safe boating course even, perhaps, before you get your new boat. They are usually run by the local Coast Guard Auxiliary or a Power Squadron in your area. As well, include the entire family. If you have young kids, it's never too early to instill in them that while their boat is lots of fun, it's also a place where they have to be careful. Not only is this kind of education something you can do together but also with everyone's collective knowledge, it just might come in handy one day. As well, it's also wise to take a First Aid/CPR class; they are easy to sit through and once you have the confidence, knowledge, and skills, your day out on the water will be that much more relaxed.

To continue, there are U.S. Coast Guard regulations that, and depending on the size of your vessel and the state in which you reside or sometimes travel to, you must adhere to in regards to the kind of equipment you are required to have onboard. Your new boat will be equipped with a dealer-supplied Coast Guard package that includes everything you need to get going. If you are purchasing a brokerage boat, have your broker ensure it is up to spec as per its required safety equipment.

To meet the requirements of all U.S. Coast Guard regulations, vessels are mandated to carry at least the minimum safety items such as proper navigational lights, fire extinguishers or automatic fire suppression system, a PFD—Personal Flotation Device, or life jacket—for each person on board, a throwable device such as a seat cushion or life ring, a bell, whistle, or horn for signaling, and visual distress signal flares.

As these requirements differ as to the size of your boat, it's best to make sure you are in compliance by checking with a copy of CG 169—usually available at your marina store or other outlets—or checking in with your local Coast Guard station or auxiliary unit. You can even set up a complimentary safety inspection with them as well. In addition, the BoatUS website (www.boatus.org) also has information to help you out and can provide nationwide emergency services when you become a member.

But there is a lot more in the way of safety awareness that you should pay attention to. No matter what size boat you have, be it kayak or superyacht,

▲ Your day out on the water with the family will be that much more enjoyable when everyone has an approved life jacket on. Unlike the ungainly yoke-type vests of years ago, today's are comfortable and stylish, and most importantly, are there to make everyone safe and secure while on board. Photo Credit: Boat US

having the right equipment aboard and knowing how to use it is one of the most important aspects of spending time out on the water.

Visual Inspection

Let's start with your boat. Always check the condition of any seacocks or thru-hull fittings as well as critical hose connections. With a new boat, this will be an easy thing to do. A quick but careful visual inspection should suffice. However, and over time, if anything looks amiss, such as signs of corrosion or cracks or weeping, swap them out for a new one. If you are running inboard engines, you may also want to give all your belts, impellers, and gaskets and seals a once over before setting out as any failure of these items can stop you dead in the water. And as with oil and oil and fuel filters, always carry spares.

Float Plan

If you are setting out for an extended time away, it's also a good idea to file a float plan with your homeport marina as well as with your destination facility. In this way, everyone will know your trip schedule and be on the lookout should anything untoward happen along the way. The MarinaLife website (www.marinalife.com) is an excellent resource to use for this very purpose.

Radio Monitoring

On this point as well, and while underway, keep a sharp ear to the VHF and a keen weather eye on conditions at least thirty-six hours ahead of your present course, just in case you are heading toward a situation you would rather not have to deal with.

As long as we've mentioned the VHF radio, everyone on board should know how to use it, especially Channel 16, the dedicated station for contacting the USCG.

Your radio should be turned on at all times while you are on the vessel and underway. It's also a good idea to have a handheld at the ready, fully charged in its cradle and also turned on. I am never without it whenever I am on my boat.

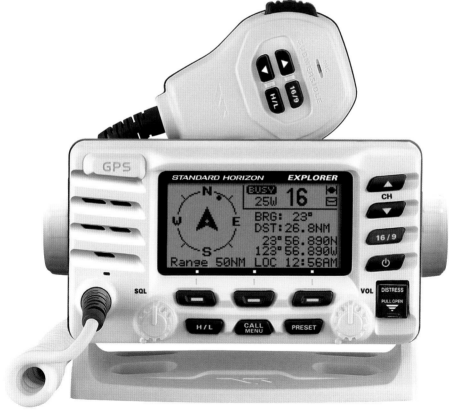

▲ Channel 16 is monitored by the USCG 24/7, and should you be facing such an emergency that requires immediate assistance, do not hesitate to make the call. Photo Credit: Standard Horizon; www.standardhorizon.com

As most of the new radios have dual channel operational capacity, it's easy to set one channel to monitor 16 and the other to your local working station for your area.

Should an emergency condition occur, someone must spring quickly into action and get on the radio. There are two situations that require swift and directed attention: the very urgent, and that presenting immediate and grave danger to life and property.

When circumstances become very urgent the following transmission, known as a Pan Pan (pronounced *pawn pawn*), should be broadcast in the following manner, in as clear, slow, and calm voice as possible, over Channel 16:

Pan Pan repeated three times.

All stations, this is VESSEL NAME (it is highly recommended to repeat VESSEL NAME twice)

We are experiencing:

Explain the type of situation, medical or mechanical

And require the following assistance:

Describe what is going on along with your present location in lat/lon, which can be read right on your GPS screen, the physical description of your vessel, and the number of people on board.

This is BOAT NAME, *over.*

You will most likely be immediately monitored and then contacted within moments from someone ready to render any kind of assistance as necessary.

Should the situation be resolved, either by assistance or your own initiatives, it's time to cancel the PAN PAN. Once again over Channel 16, the following is said:

PAN PAN, PAN PAN

HELLO ALL STATIONS, HELLO ALL STATIONS

THIS IS . . . BOAT NAME . . . AND IT IS . . . give the present time . . .

CANCEL PAN PAN

THIS IS . . . BOAT NAME . . . OUT

With a situation that you feel is untenable and quickly spiraling out of control in such a manner as to put both someone on board as well as your boat in a critical and perilous situation, it's time for a MAYDAY.

A word of caution here. Sending a MAYDAY indicates a significant event is taking place and is one of those resolute and steadfast rules of the sea that no one messes with. The responders who answer the call are putting their lives on the line, as well as those needing assistance, and being sent out on a false action is taken very seriously with harsh fines and penalties for those partaking in such dangerous behavior.

If a MAYDAY is necessary to be broadcast over Channel 16, again in as clear, slow, and calm voice as possible, the following format is generally accepted:

MAYDAY repeated three times

This is . . . VESSEL NAME . . . repeated three times

MAYDAY . . . VESSEL NAME . . . MY POSITION IS . . . use GPS information along with present compass heading, approximate running time since you left and any well-known landmark, inlet, coastal area, or navigational aid that can assist the responders to find you in the quickest way

The nature of my emergency is . . . (AS DETAILED AS POSSIBLE) . . . and we require . . . (THE KIND OF ASSISTANCE NECESSARY). We have . . . NUMBER OF PEOPLE ON BOARD INCLUDING ANY CHILDREN AS WELL AS THE CONDITION OF ANYONE WHO HAS SUFFERED INJURY . . . and the following safety equipment . . .

BOAT NAME *is a . . .* GIVE A FULL DESCRIPTION INCLUDING LENGTH, HULL COLOR, TYPE OF BOAT, AND ANY OUTSTANDING FEATURES THAT WILL AID RESPONDERS IN VISUALLY LOCATING YOU.

WE WILL BE MONITORING AND STANDING BY ON CHANNEL 16

BOAT NAME . . . OVER

With a MAYDAY call, there will be an almost immediate response to your emergency and hopefully, aid and comfort will arrive as quickly as possible.

Let's hope you never have to use either of these transmissions but just in case, please make this routine as familiar to you as possible and share the information with several others who are with you. It's that important.

A final word on your VHF radio: it is not for social calls. Use your cell phone for that. Your shipboard radio is for monitoring traffic, communicating your intentions to another vessel should that be necessary, and for emergencies.

Pre-Trip Briefing

If you are traveling with any family, friends, and kids who are not familiar with being out on the water, take the time to go through all the safety features and procedures aboard before you cast off. If you have a pet, it's best to keep it in sight and have an appropriate life jacket and even a tether on it at all times. And finally, never overload your boat. It is one of the leading causes of accidents and can have serious and even grave repercussions.

Fuel

Keep your fuel tanks full and know where your next fill up will be and how long it is going to take you to get there. When taking on fuel, and whether you have a diesel engine or gasoline power, turn off all your machinery, shut off your battery switches, fans, and any other equipment that could produce an electrical spark, and close all hatches, ports, and doors to prevent any fumes from finding their way inside. Of course, this is not the time to light up a smoke—you know you shouldn't be doing it anyway but I won't get up on that soap box right now—and know the capacity of your fuel tank and how much you are putting in. Remember, fuel expands so leave a little room for it to do so.

Here's hoping your next outing is a safe and enjoyable one. With a little extra planning, taking any bad weather indicators or forecasts seriously, becoming familiar with the local knowledge in your area as well as that during your travels, asking your dockmates for help when necessary, and being always ready, you can enjoy your time on the water with some extra confidence and peace of mind.

10 Brokers, Surveys & Surveyors, Loans & Clubs

"My escape is to just get in a boat and disappear on the water."

—Carl Hiaasen, Writer

*S*o, now that we've been through enough chapters in this book to enable you to have a fairly clear picture of what you may be up against in your quest to owning your first boat, let's now take the dream, along with the glossy brochures, magazines, and online searches, and set them aside for a moment in order to deal with the realities of paying for it.

As with real estate, where *location, location, location* is the mantra, and if you don't have the disposable income to make it happen on your own, when looking to secure a broker, getting a survey, and financing a boat, it's *reputation, reputation, reputation*.

Brokers

Therefore, let's begin the discussion with the broker. It is my very strong conviction that any search be undertaken with as much due diligence as possible.

As you already know, the lifestyle is an expense and in order to protect your investment when considering a brokerage boat, you should always lead with your better judgment and have a clear grasp on your economics instead of what you are hoping to have happen.

I say go with the top brokerage businesses in the industry. HMY, MarineMax, Galati Yachts, GilmanYacht Sales, Bluewater Yacht Sales, and YachtWorld just to name a very few on a very long list.

Your search, as so many others do in this technological age, begins on the Internet. As you set the process in motion, put aside an hour or so—longer if you have the time—each day to peruse the many, many, many offerings.

For example, check out this screen shot on the next page from MarineMax.

One of the most respected boat dealers offering brokerage services, they have locations throughout the US. Navigating the search page, and much like the others you will find as you look for your boat, you are asked to fill in the information that will help narrow things down a bit. Once you do, you will receive a listing of all available boats that satisfies your profile. Most big brokerage concerns offer a kind of one-stop shopping: boat, loan, and insurance. If you are keen and comfortable with something like this, it can help streamline the process for you with, if nothing else, peace of mind.

You should then create a file of all those boats that

1. fit into your budget
2. have the layout and equipment you are looking for
3. hopefully have had one owner
4. were well taken care of and presented in a manner that shows they have been maintained to high standards

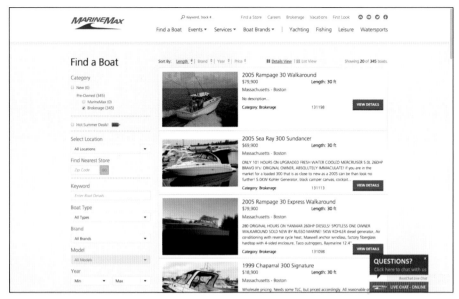

▲ Easy to navigate and search the sizable offerings in your size and price range, using MarineMax's services can narrow down your choices to exactly what you are looking for. Photo Credit: MarineMax

5. have verifiable hours
6. a checkable service record of all engine maintenance and any engine or structural repairs as well as a recent survey
7. be relatively new to the brokerage market since a boat listed for a very long time will most likely not be on your short list
8. be the kind of investment you will get the most out of, especially when you are ready to get something just a bit bigger.

I'm sure there are more but this should be a good start.

But before we delve into these unchartered waters, let us pause for a slight but important on-point diversion. Well, actually a little bit left of center as it were.

A Thought on Names and Superstitions

While we have had the discussion in Chapter 2 on naming your new boat, just what do you do with a brokerage boat you have purchased that already has a name across her transom or festooned upon her bows?

Take heed, my friends, should you be faced with such a dilemma, there is a solution to the problem. You see, besides any lost tribe of humans still living in the deep, deep forests of South America and who have never seen one vestige of modern civilization as yet, there is no more superstitious group of beings on the planet than mariners.

▲ A very personal statement of who is the king of this nautical castle . . . or so he would like to believe.

Where the root of this somewhat irrational, illogical, specious, and unsound reasoning has come from through the ages on a wide variety of subjects and concerns swirling about being on, in, under, and around the water is in itself worthy of volumes of academic study. My own experience with just one of these beliefs was pointed out to me with a swift and firm cuff on the back of the head. Let me explain with yet another short digression.

Years back, I was part of a delivery crew bringing up a yacht from a shipyard in North Florida and with three captains on board, along with two deckhands, we relegated ourselves to eight-hour shifts at the wheel.

We were seasoned and capable with all sorts of wheel time on boats of all sizes and shapes. One of our cabal, the most senior, was a gruff and tough tugboat captain with as much water in his wake as anyone I had ever known.

On one particular watch along a stretch of the Intracoastal, we had to duck in from the ocean due to some rather nasty weather and instead of putting our charge through the sloppy conditions, decided to seek calmer waters for a spell. As I settled in at the helm, I absentmindedly began a soft whistle with no particular tune in mind. It was just a wandering whisper of a melody, not going anywhere and not coming from any particular place.

The sudden and immediate open-handed smack to the back of my head, delivered by a quintet of digits the thickness of kielbasa, quickly ended my drifting and promptly put a stop to my roving piece of aimless and pointless attempt at any musical ability. In junior high school, and after many failed attempts at tapping the triangle, I had trouble with the comb and wax paper and was instead relegated to cleaning out the chalk-filled erasers of the music teacher by slapping a basketful of them against a wall in the schoolyard during music class. So be it. Not everybody is hard-wired that way.

"Whistlin' in the wheelhouse brings up the wind," said the beefy Captain Tug, standing a few feet behind me and off to my port side.

"I didn't know," I said as I kind of rubbed the place where I still felt the remnants of where his bear-paw of a hand had landed and then, as quickly, alighted.

"Well, now you do," was all he came back with. And that was that.

You see, in olden days, becalmed sailors whistled whether at the wheel, swabbing the decks, chained in the fo'c'sle, or just about to be keelhauled. This warbling was believed to bring up the wind.

Of course, centuries later, since the last thing some of us motorized boaters need is a blustery day—sail boaters need not heed this particular fallaciousness as they often require some sort of snotty blow to get them from Point A to Point B and even perhaps back again lest they turn on their engines to cover some ground at the very least; so for the rag baggers amongst us, tweet and twitter away to your heart's desire. So be it.

For the rest of us, trilling aboard is absolutely verboten. However, if any of you power boaters happen to forget yourselves, as I did—to this day shipmates, I always catch myself before whistling up a tune while aboard, not so much for violating the superstition but more for the expectation of Captain Tug giving me another what-for—and by chance do pucker up and blow, merely spit overboard in the direction from which the wind is coming, and any errant gust will hasten itself to disappear. Don't forget to duck or feint one way or the other lest your expectorate hit you on the way back.

If it does, take a bucket of water from the ocean, lake, river, or bathtub you might be boating in at the time and douse the spot where you were hit. If it lands on your face, you can't just wash the spot off. Instead, you'll have to dump the whole bucket over your head. Of course there's a more salty approach but again, this is a family book.

Sorry for drifting away like that but back to the point. It's bad luck to change the name of a boat. Well, what if you don't like the name of the boat you're contemplating buying? Or, perish the thought, already own? *Tripe Stew. Muck & Mire. Regurgitation. Skid Marx. Haggis.*

Yes friends, these and others, some way too blue to make it into print for this collection, are names I've seen adorning the transom, often in gold leaf and lavishly illustrated, of many a craft.

If you really can't stand your just-purchased dreamboat's present name—or if is so offensive as to be a deal breaker—you can change it without fear of reprisal. But do it only in the following manner lest you stir up a heap of trouble.

First, you will have to ceremoniously obliterate the old name everywhere you find it. For example, run a piece of very fine sandpaper once lightly across the transom—don't worry, your new name will be going there—or if the bows and elsewhere are so adorned, there as well.

If there is a ship's log aboard—logs are often kept by new owners for maintenance schedules and other important information—or a life ring, raft, salt and pepper shakers, bar naps, glasses—as in the set with "*The Smiths,*" written on them along with those little red, white, and blue nautical life rings for example; any *The Smiths Welcome You Aboard* signs, and so on, take a pen, pencil, or marker and draw a single line through the name everywhere it appears.

Continue doing this throughout the boat, making a mark that in some way deletes the odious moniker. I mean, come on, you can't keep this stuff unless your initials match or names are the same. Right? You can even cover the name with a piece of black electrical tape or that cool blue or green painter's tape. Anything that shows you are, at the very least, trying to cover it up. Be creative.

Next take a piece of paper and write the soon-to-be-exorcised name on it. No script or cursive letters please, only stand-alone, block letters. Lower case is okay. Fold the paper up and place it in a small cardboard or wooden box. If none is available, a paper bag will do just fine. Burn the box, or bag, completely until there are only ashes left. Scoop up the residue and take it to the water's edge. Throw the remains into the sea on an outgoing tide. If you live on a lake, do it at night and only during a new moon. For you river dwellers, send the remains downstream.

You may now change the name everywhere on your vessel without fear of irking the ire of any mischievous water sprite. And of course the monogrammed towels will have to go.

The Survey

So, where were we? Oh yes, brokerage boats, surveys, and surveyors.

Once you have located the boat or boats you think you may want to have a go at, your next move is to have the boat surveyed; that, gone over by an expert who is your advocate and is not in any way connected to the seller, broker, agent, or dealership.

One of the more important aspects of navigating the brokerage market is being able to find (a) the right broker and (b) a reputable surveyor for both the boat and its machinery.

Some factors to consider when dealing with a broker begin with honesty. This can be a tough call sometimes. To me, it all gets back to reputation.

Word of mouth. Dock buzz. Go with the pros. Top echelons in the biz. Status and standing in the industry is set very high and those that cannot rise to the occasion, or who prove to be disreputable, quickly disappear.

Several good barometric readings include how long have they been in business, what their track record is, and any strong or related background experience such as being a veteran delivery or boat captain. Are they specialists in a particular sector? Big boat project managers or small boat authority? Did you have an *"I didn't know that"* moment where you found out something important you did not know before beginning the process? And I think you always have to go with your feelings; am I comfortable with this person or organization? If not, it may be time to move on to someone or somewhere else.

You might also want to consider the professional organizations they are affiliated with such as the Yacht Brokers Association of America (YBAA) and Certified Professional Yacht Broker (CPYB) among others. Having this kind of accreditation is always a good sign.

Let's discuss surveyors. This person, because of his or her extensive background experience in boat design, construction, machinery, operations, and many other factors, will be able, once they have completed a thorough going over of the vessel you have your eye on, present you with a detailed, unbiased report of all aspects, defects, and recommendations they have found during their inspection. As with working with a broker, it is reputation, reputation, and reputation. Make sure you get reliable and verifiable references and pick only the best.

The Society of Accredited Marine Surveyors (SAMS), is an organization of professional marine surveyors who have come together to promote the good image and general well-being of their chosen profession.

Accredited Marine Surveyor members are surveyors who have accumulated time in the profession, and have proven the technical skills necessary for designation as AMS. They are expected to follow a course of continuing education to maintain their accreditation. Members are guided by a code of ethics and are encouraged to participate in other organizations relative to the marine field. (www.societyofaccreditedmarinesurveyors.com)

The National Association of Marine Surveyors (NAMS) is another organization that you should consider when looking into vetting a surveyor. With Apprenticeship, Associate, and rigorous certification programs, NAMS personnel have a wide range of expertise throughout the industry.

As with SAMS, this organization adheres to a strict code of ethics and holds each and every one of its surveyors to high standards of professionalism. (www.namsglobal.org)

Insurance and Loans

While lying somewhere between your home and car insurance, protecting your boat, and you and yours, can be different. Property damage, liability, damage, towing, storms, vandalism, theft, fire, medical payments, pollution from a fuel spill, agreed and market values, out of water time, storage on land, in a dock, or at home, uninsured boat owners coverage, and so much more has to be taken into consideration that unless you are with the right person, you can be open to a host of ills better not dealt with and to be avoided at all costs.

As with everything we have been discussing here, go with the best in the business. Yacht World (www.yachtworld.com), the National Boat Owners Association (www.nboat.com), and our friends at Discover Boating (www.discoverboating.com) and BoatUS (www.boatus.com) can also be of invaluable assistance in navigating the muck and mire that can often be found in this area.

With proper insurance, make sure your broker explains each and every detail of the policy you are interested in. Not taking the time during this phase of the process can lead to some dicey things going forward. If something is not clear, or if it seems not in your interest, and you do not get a clear and precise answer, it may be time to move on to someone else.

Again, if your brokerage agent can supply these necessary items, you may want to stay with them but only if they are with one of the best firms in the industry. Which, of course, is who you should be with anyway. Check out what both the BoatUS and Discover Boating sites have in the way of some excellent information for you to peruse. I strongly suggest you utilize it. And remember, everything has some wiggle room and is negotiable.

As far as boat loans are concerned, and as we have discussed with finding a broker and a surveyor, this is not the place to take any shortcuts with Savvy Steve's Quick Financing & Loan Company.

Shop your needs around with the top financial institutions in the business. If you attend any of the many boat shows, you will most likely be able to discuss things with in-the-know personnel from Key Bank (www.keybank.com) and Sun Trust (www.suntrust.com), and Geico—just three of the many fine, reputable places you can find someone to speak with and enjoy a high-degree of confidence in. And if you are friendly with your local banker, you might want to run this by them as well.

As with everything we have been discussing here, go with the best in the business. Yacht World (www.yachtworld.com), the National Boat Owners Association (www.nboat.com), and our friends at Discover Boating (www.discoverboating.com) and BoatUS (www.boatus.com) can also be of invaluable assistance in navigating the muck and mire that can often be found in this area.

Clubs

There is one more avenue to go down in your search for a particular boat that perhaps is out of your economic reach right now or due to your present lifestyle, is just not doable with restrictions on time and location. While both might change, still boat ownership at this point in your life is too much of a reach.

Enter the concept of the Freedom Boat Club. Established in Sarasota, Florida, in 1989, Freedom has grown to become a viable and affordable alternative to boat ownership for first timers as well as seasoned mariners alike.

The idea is simple: With a one-time entry fee and monthly dues, a member will be entitled to unlimited use of the vessels in the club fleet. They do not own any of the boats nor do they incur any service or storage fees. One simply goes on an online site, makes a reservation, and shows up to go boating. The management service takes care of all service and maintenance.

The Club also provides instruction for newbies as well as reciprocal participation in any other location for yearly members. The boats themselves are always kept in tip-top shape with a regular rotation of new boats coming into the system every three years. Other amenities include dock parties, dinners, group excursions, and even fishing seminars.

The Freedom Boat Club has more than eighty-six franchise and corporate club locations in nineteen states and is growing. They maintain a healthy ratio of boats to members so that all its participants will be able to go boating. (www. freedomboatclub.com)

▲ Membership in the Freedom Boat Club gets you and your family and friends access to a wide variety of boats and activities. Photo Credit: Freedom Boat Club

▲ Well-organized, supportive, and very social, getting out on your boat is just one of the perks with your Freedom Boat Club membership. Photo Credit: Freedom Boat Club

11. Resources

"The way a team plays as a whole determines its success. You may have the greatest bunch of individual stars in the world, but if they don't play together, the club won't be worth a dime."

– George Herman "Babe" Ruth, Baseball Player

aybe it's because getting out on the water can be both intimidating and exhilarating at the same time that there is a deep wealth of supportive organizations and resources that boaters can use.

I have found throughout my career, there is nothing more sustaining and comforting than the people I have met along the way. And perhaps most important are those who have helped out, had a bit more information and knowledge, and were ready to jump aboard with wrench, hose, spare part, or whatever else was necessary to assist when and if necessary. It comes with the territory and no matter where I visited or stayed I found this to be true.

Indeed, as the more personal side of boating takes care of its own so does the industry look after us with a host of helpful organizations and groups dedicated to being there with all sorts of useful information and the kind of assistance that will help you stay on course. A simple phone call or email to the right group will open up an entire support program to get you headed in the right direction.

The following is a rather comprehensive list and covers most of what you may be looking for.

Organizations

BoatUS

Boat Owners Association of The United States (BoatUS) has been looking after the interests of recreational boaters since 1966. They are the nation's largest organization of recreational boat owners, with over half a million dues-paying members.

BoatUS provides a diverse offering of marine services for the recreational boater, including insuring over $8 billion worth of boats; operating the largest on the water towing fleet, TowBoatUS; representing boaters' interests on Capitol Hill; providing financing for boat-buyers; creating quality boat graphics and lettering; publishing the most widely circulated boating publication, *BoatUS Magazine*; acting as a mediator through their Consumer Protection Bureau, and more.

Take the time to visit their website (www.boatus.com) for some of the most comprehensive information available for all types of boaters; from the novice, entry-level right up to the veteran mariner, there is truly something for everyone.

National Marine Manufacturers Association

The National Marine Manufacturers Association (NMMA) is the nation's leading trade association representing boat, marine engine, and accessory manufacturers. Collectively, NMMA members manufacture an estimated 80 percent of marine products used in North America and is a unifying force and powerful voice for the recreational boating industry, working to strengthen and grow boating and protect the interests of its member companies.

To that end, NMMA:

* Represents the industry on public policy issues, advocating at state and federal levels to protect the interests of the marine industry and the users of products
* Collects, analyzes, and distributes industry, economic, and market data; NMMA is the industry's primary source of recreational boating research, statistics, and technical data.
* Promotes recreational boating through consumer outreach
* Provides information and represents the industry's interests to the media and other public entities.
* Produces boat and sport shows in key North American markets to provide quality sales venues for exhibitors and consumers
* Co-owns/produces the trade event IBEX (International Boat Builders' Exhibition and Conference) to generate business opportunities for marine companies
* Works to create opportunities overseas; offers information and services to help members expand into the global marketplace
* Maintains boat, trailer, and oil certification programs to promote safety and help manufacturers produce quality products
* Assists the industry in continuously improving customer satisfaction with the purchase, delivery, product, use, and after-sale experiences through CSI (Consumer Satisfaction Index): www.nmma.org

U.S. Coast Guard

The U.S. Coast Guard is one of the five armed forces of the United States and the only military organization within the Department of Homeland Security.

Since 1790 the Coast Guard has safeguarded our Nation's maritime interests and environment around the world. The Coast Guard is an adaptable, responsive military force of maritime professionals whose broad legal authorities, capable assets, geographic diversity, and expansive partnerships provide a persistent presence along our rivers, in the ports, littoral regions, and on the high seas. Coast Guard presence and impact is local, regional, national, and international. These attributes make the Coast Guard a unique instrument of maritime safety, security, and environmental stewardship.

▲ A familiar sight on the waterways of the United States is this USCG Patrol Boat.

Today's U.S. Coast Guard, with nearly forty-two thousand men and women on active duty, is a unique force that carries out an array of civil and military responsibilities touching almost every facet of the U.S. maritime environment: www.uscg.mil

Coast Guard Auxiliary

The mission of the Auxiliary is to promote and improve Recreational Boating Safety and to provide trained crews and facilities to augment the Coast Guard

and enhance safety and security of our country's ports, waterways, and coastal regions. The volunteers also support Coast Guard operational, administrative, and logistical requirements as well.

The Auxiliary operates in:

- Safety and Security Patrols
- Search and Rescue
- Mass Casualty or Disasters
- Pollution Response & Patrols
- Homeland Security
- Recreational Boating Safety
- Commercial Fishing and Vessel Exams
- Platforms for Boarding Parties
- Recruit for all service in the Coast Guard

The Auxiliary has units in all fifty states, Puerto Rico, the Virgin Islands, American Samoa, and Guam. Under the direct authority of the U.S. Department of Homeland Security via the Commandant of the U.S. Coast Guard, the Auxiliary's internally operating levels are broken down into four organizational levels: Flotilla, Division, District, and National.

While the men and women of the USCG Auxiliary perform many important and supportive functions, two of the more important ones are to provide Boating Safety Education and Vessel Safety Checks.

U.S. Coast Guard Auxiliary boating courses provide instruction to boaters at all levels, from the fundamental to the advanced. Experienced and knowledgeable instructors committed to the highest standards of the U.S. Coast Guard teach the classes. From safety to navigation to boating skills, seamanship, GPS, weather, your VHF radio, as well as instruction for young adults and children, you will find an enriching program that will make your boating more fun and a lot safer. For further information about upcoming courses near you, please visit www.cgaux.org/boatinged/ for the complete list.

VSC

A Vessel Safety Check (VSC) is performed at your boat—ranging in locations from boat to your driveway. A vessel safety check usually takes fifteen to thirty minutes, depending upon the size of your boat.

Vessels passing safety checks are awarded a U.S. Coast Guard/Auxiliary Decal that informs the Coast Guard, the Auxiliary, harbor police, any local sheriff or harbor patrol, as well as other boating law enforcement and safety agency of your passing inspection and that your boat was in full compliance with all Federal and State boating laws during the safety check for that year.

Best of all, every Vessel Safety Check is 100 percent free of charge. If your boat does not pass, no citation is issued at that time. Instead, you are provided a written report in how to correct any discrepancies.

The Vessel Safety Check is to assist you in making sure that your boating experience is enjoyable and safe. The peace of mind that your boat meets federal safety standards and that in an emergency you will have the necessary equipment to save lives and summon help.

In many cases boating insurance agencies offer discounts for vessels that undergo a Vessel Safety Check every year. All decals and safety checks are void December 31st of year they are inspected, they are also void should the operator/owner fail to maintain the vessel's equipment or the vessel itself to the standard at the time of the safety check.

WHAT TYPE OF ITEMS ARE CHECKED?

- Life jackets
- Registration and numbering
- Navigation lights
- Ventilation
- Fire extinguishers
- Distress signals (flares, horn, etc.)
- Battery cover and connections

All these items are currently required by state and federal laws and, if missing or non-operating, can result in a citation if the Coast Guard inspects your vessel.

You can schedule an inspection by using the link when you visit the site. The closest volunteer vessel examiner will be found within thirty miles of your location and a request will be made that they contact you and set up a Vessel Safety Check for your boat: www.cgaux.org

U.S. Power Squadrons

The United States Power Squadrons (USPS) is the world's largest recreational boating organization with more than thirty-five thousand members. For more than a hundred years, the connected organizations have worked to make the water a safer place for your, your family and friends through boating education, civic service, and fellowship.

With the United States Power Squadrons, you can improve your boating skills and knowledge online, in the classroom with certified instructors, or outdoors with hands-on training. By joining America's premier boating organization, you can have fun with other boaters on the water and on land.

USPS offers a full range of educational experiences for both novice and experienced boaters. Expert teachers lead a variety of comprehensive courses and short seminars to advance your know-how of seamanship and boat handling, piloting and navigation, boat systems maintenance, weather, sailing, cruise planning, and other topics specifically created to meet the needs of today's boater.

With USPS, you have complete flexibility in scheduling your education through classroom instruction, online courses, and on-the-water skills training.

Through hundreds of local squadrons, you can enjoy personal interaction with certified instructors, get in-depth answers to your boating questions, and benefit from group learning and interaction.

- Get hands-on training and skills development in boat handling and other topics related to your coursework.
- Online education is convenient and you can learn as your time allows.

USPS offers in-depth courses (usually six to eight weeks), focused two-hour seminars, and skills certification in inland, coastal, and offshore navigation and boat operation. Mix and match to suit your boating education needs.

USPS members enjoy many affordable and comprehensive programs that increase their boating knowledge and skills, have more fun, and connect with fellow boaters through a variety of educational and social activities. With USPS membership, you receive:

- Boating education to help you become a more competent and safer boater
- A wide variety of comprehensive courses and informative seminars to advance your skill and knowledge in boat operation and maintenance
- Savings of 20 to 50 percent or more on these courses and seminars
- Flexibility in scheduling your education through classroom instruction, online courses, and on-the-water skills training
- Interaction with a group of experienced boaters who know how to have fun—raft-ups, cruises, picnics, and get-togethers
- Savings on boat insurance and many other products and services

The only requirements for membership are a keen interest in boating-related activities and an eagerness to meet like-minded people. You don't need a boat to join: www.usps.org

NBOA

It's a fact of life that getting the proper insurance coverage is a must and your new boat is going to need the proper boat insurance.

The National Boat Owners Association (NBOA) strives to provide every boater with the best insurance available, while also accommodating every aspect of the boating lifestyle.

Whether you are searching for an affordable quote, comparing boat insurance quotes, financing a boat, searching for the right towing program, or simply shopping for the latest in life jackets and other safety equipment, NBOA is the one-stop shopping experience for boaters nationwide.

As a boat insurance company for over thirty years, and as one of the largest boat insurance agencies in the country, NBOA works closely with several exclusive A-rated insurance carriers to ensure you get the most comprehensive boat insurance coverage at the best possible rate. From PWC insurance to yacht insurance to powerboat insurance; from inland to Bahamas coverage; and from life jackets to chart maps, NBOA can provide you and your boat with everything you need to get out on the water—and return safely.

While membership is not necessary to receive boat insurance, becoming a National Boat Owners Association member is easy, affordable, and can save you time and money.

With your NBOA membership you get a comprehensive towing supplement, receive discounts on the wide-ranging Boat Equipment Store, and collect expert tips and news from marine industry leaders. It's the company's way of showing their customers that they want to cover them with more than just boating insurance.

In addition to offering the best coverage for boat owners nationwide, NBOA also works closely with boat dealers to ensure the most reliable service at the point of sale: www.nboat.com

Sea Tow

Years back, I had the pleasure of meeting and getting to know Captain Joe Frohnhoefer. A big, gregarious, smiling gentleman, Captain Joe, the founder of Sea Tow Services, was always concerned with safety on the water.

With that in mind, in 2007, he set up the Sea Tow Foundation, a non-profit dedicated to help prevent boating related accidents, injuries, and unfortunately, deaths. The mission is simple: to promote safe boating practices that directly reduce accidents, fatalities, and property damage related to recreational boating. To that end, its supporters and those who donate and volunteers help to spread the word, educate, and raise funds with such worthwhile programs as the Designated Skipper, life jacket drive and loaner, as well as grants and fellowships.

With Captain Joe's passing in 2015, his legacy of caring and concern will most assuredly continue through the actions of both Sea Tow services and the Sea Tow Foundation: www.seatow.com; www.boatingsafety.com

ABA

The American Boating Association (ABA) is dedicated to improving the safety, affordability, environmental cleanliness, and growth of the boating lifestyle.

With member services including a host of benefits, boating information including safety, maintenance, and cruising destinations among a long list of others, boat loans and insurance, resources such as manufacturers, dealers, surveyors, boat tests and evaluations, education and laws, weather, news, travel safety and other varied and interesting topics: www.americanboating.org

MarinaLife

MarinaLife is one of those resources that once you use it, with its easy-to-navigate and jam-packed-with-useful-information format, you will be a regular visitor and participant.

Just about anything you want to know about getting from here to there . . . and perhaps somewhere else—is readily available.

You can locate, review, and make a reservation at a marina or create a cruise plan with a mileage calculator and check out local destination features. Resources include the site's Ask The Captain component, where you can get cruising tips, finance and insurance information, where to get fuel, maintenance issues, and navigation and weather data.

Other notable offerings include a cruising club, magazine, relevant video presentations, featured destinations, and comprehensive reviews: www.marinalife.com

Discover Boating

Discover Boating is a comprehensive online service that covers almost every aspect of the boating lifestyle and is an invaluable tool to networking in order to get the kind of information you are seeking.

As a buyer, you can explore the kind and type of boat you are looking for, get directed and pertinent insurance and financing tips, find out about engines, maintenance, day or extended cruising, where to find certified boat dealers, trailering, accessories, fishing, stories, articles, videos, environmental issues, and a very long list of other opportunities and features: www.discoverboating.com

National Marine Electronics Association

This important association is responsible for the facilitation and support of the development and implementation of standards for the entire marine electronics industry. No small task as this includes government regulations for both recreational and regulated vessels.

With its extensive and rigorous training program, education and certification of the NMEA's technicians and installers is a top priority. Training events occur around the country as well as in Canada, the UK, and Europe. The Master

Dealer program, with its accompanying logo, indicates that the company has the expertise, training, and dedication to achieve this accolade.

Technical announcements are made concerning the latest news and can include VHF radios, public notices from the FCC, USCG information, and lots of other important and noteworthy updates: www.nmea.org.

American Boat & Yacht Council

Here's a statistic from the American Boat & Yacht Council (ABYC) that deserves your attention: 90 percent of boats on the water are built to ABYC standards.

With not enough laws within the Code of Federal Regulations (CFR) governing the construction standards for recreational boat construction here in the States except those for fire extinguishers, life jackets, nav lights and distress signals, the government has left it up to the marine industry to self-regulate itself in regards to safe and prudent practices in this sector.

The American Boat & Yacht Council was formed by members of the Motorboat and Yacht Advisory Panel of the U.S. Coast Guard's Merchant Marine Council and was incorporated on February 1, 1954, in New York State as a not-for-profit, 501(c)(3) corporation.

According to the ABYC, the importance of setting up standards and technical informational reports that cover major boating systems industry wide, along with the development of annual reviews, can be seen in the significant reduction in the number of boating accidents over the past six decades. Standard areas include construction, galley stoves, fire fighting equipment, refrigeration and air conditioning, gasoline fumes and carbon monoxide detection systems, generators, battery charges and inverters, ignition protection, batteries, AC and DC electrical systems, ventilation, boat load capacity, fuel and power systems, lightning protection, thru-hull fittings and drain plugs, among a very long list of other important and critical aspects for the industry.

ABYC is on the leading edge of the movement toward greater reliance upon standards that improve boating safety for the recreational boating community. Offering seminars, workshops and technician certification courses ABYC is instrumental in increasing the level of knowledge and professionalism throughout the boating industry: www.abycinc.org

12. The Greening of the Boating Industry

"Green issues at last are attracting serious attention, owing to critically important links between the environment and the economy, health, and our security."
—Sylvia Earle, Oceanographer

"Water and air, the two essentials on which all life depends, have become global garbage cans."
—Jacques Yves Cousteau, Explorer, Diver, Author, Environmentalist, Icon

his chapter might well be called The Shape of Things to Come or The Buzz or perhaps even The Hum.

And just to kick things off, here is an excerpt from a forum thread I picked up on while researching this topic. It's kind of funny and easy to imagine:

"I have been doing some drawings using an 18-volt cordless drill and a 90″ drive. I would like to build a prototype but don't want to spend a lot on proof or a design model. Maybe this winter? It might be what the canoe and kayak people are looking for?"

Then this response:

"For a little boat, you might just try a cordless drill as-is. Attach a prop to the drill and hold it underwater. Just might work fine in water. Haven't tried it myself."

Okay, so I don't think the drill thing is going to work. Better scrap that idea and move on. But I couldn't resist this last one to kind of dog the hatch here:

"Also wanted to add that many power tools will also operate just fine on DC rather than AC power. So for example, you can take a beefy angle grinder and run it on 24v battery power, which would probably spin it at an RPM more useful for a prop than 120v."

We've seen it before. A need addressed usually results in some sort of a solution, however circuitous or less travelled the path might be. Kind of like that old chestnut of a saying: necessity is the mother of invention.

I even remember way back, again referring to my yard snipe days, hearing some of the old timers lament about this new "LORAN thing."

"What the hell's wrong with a watch, a compass, and a chart, fer Chrissakes?" was the usual invective followed of course by a litany of salty abuses, a string of *"I remember whens"* and various mumblings about the current state of events and what the world is coming to. What fun.

The boating industry itself, usually a bit reticent to change, most likely due to economic considerations in my opinion, has indeed heard the call and has taken many steps to "clean up its act." After all, in an industry where everything it utilizes in its manufacturing processes is tied to petroleum-based products and by-products, trying to make that happen is a daunting undertaking at the very least.

However, with new, innovative, and carefully designed goods, systems, environmentally compliant and more energy efficient, cleaner burning engines, building techniques utilizing vacuum bagging, self-contained paint rooms, and superior air-handling equipment in the shops and factory facilities, and in the buildings themselves among other positive changes, things are moving in the right direction.

Electric Power

But certainly, with today's geopolitical climate being what it is, and whether you ascribe to any doomsday theories about the end of oil supplies or not, or whatever level of tree hugger you might be, the often rollercoaster and volatile price at the pump coupled with a keen awareness of the need for environmental considerations in the wake of recent oil spills and the alarming rate of both land and sea pollution is certainly driving research into not only alternative fuel sources and sustainability, but in the direction of energy replacements as well. Enter the idea of harnessing electric power for boat engines.

First, as I have done throughout when it comes to over-technical information, let's skip all the intensive physics lessons concerning electrons and protons, electromagnetism, or the laws of Newton, Ampere, Ohm, and Kirschhoff, and instead cut right to the chase.

Basically, an electric motor takes the electrical energy it requires, such as that produced by a battery, or enhanced/backed up by solar power, and turns it into movement. So instead of an internal combustion engine under the cowling burning fossil fuel and sending out exhaust, there is an electric motor turning the driveshaft to move your boat through the water.

▲ As far back as the 1800s, and even when most environmental issues were not even considered, Elco was pioneering clean, non-polluting energy. Photo Credit: Elco Motor Yachts

The concept is not new. You could say, as far as the boating industry is concerned, it began in Chicago at the World's Columbian Exposition on the afternoon of May 1, 1893, where well over one million passengers would take rides on fifty-five electric powered boats designed and built by the Electric Launch Company, better known as Elco, over the course of the event.

For this discussion, most of the impact has shown up in the outboard engine sector. Today, there are several electric engine manufacturers in the forefront of the technology whose designs, in some applications, offer a sensible, quiet, economical, and non-polluting alternative to internal combustion power.

ReGen Nautic

Let's start with Ft. Lauderdale-based ReGen Nautic. The company has been making quite a splash with its 180- and 130-hp, fully electric outboard engines. Joining forces with Campion Boats, Canada's largest producer of fiberglass boats, they already have a Chase 550 Bow Rider and 180-hp electric engine off to a Swiss dealer.

"This technology has to start somewhere and we feel it is with us," said ReGen's president and CEO Pierre Caouette. "Among the most important aspects are our concerns about the safety systems we design into our products, ones that are well-understood by our company. Improved battery technology

▲ Riding the wave of future alternative power, ReGen offers clean, non-polluting electric outboard engines.

is moving forward and we are positioning ReGen Nautic to be there when it happens."

The ReGen 180, with its 38.4 kW lithium-ion battery bank, has gone for about twenty minutes at near peak power before having to go in for a charge. "With hi/lo operation, we've gotten two hours before recharge. And the boat has easily pulled water skiers and wake boarders," said Caouette. However, it may make sense in a more practical application, such as that for a megayacht tender, where the engine can be easily recharged by a big boat genset system, or in a multi-engine configuration instead of running gasoline-powered engines for slow bell operations when entering a harbor or navigating a long stretch of no-wake zones: www.regennautic.com

Torqueedo

Winner of a prestigious DAME Innovation Award at the 2015 METS gathering in Amsterdam, Torqueedo, the German electric outboard motor company, with thirteen offerings from 1- to 15-hp, is relying on its new 80-hp DEEP BLUE engine to propel it forward and into a strong position in this market.

According to the company's fact sheet, the DEEP BLUE System incorporates top to bottom specifically designed engineering. Among other features are a matched gearbox, and a waterproof venting and breathing seal, this to prevent any moisture from affecting the battery, compensate for temperature variants, and, in the unlikely event, to safely vent any gases. The connection box is the system's nerve center connecting all the electrical and signal cables while providing a connection for two to four batteries. And an on-board computer and touchscreen display, with fourteen different screens, covers a wide range of information including GPS-based range and battery charge status. The company

▲ Torqueedo's Deep Blue has been designed especially for the marine environment. Photo Credit: Torqueedo

has a fairly comprehensive and informational website and should this particular technology interest you, you are urged to visit: www.torqueedo.com

Pure Watercraft

This one is truly a fine example of keeping up with and perhaps even staying ahead of the curve. Taking his inspiration from Elon Musk's forward thinking entry into providing an alternative to the imperious sphere of gasoline and diesel powered cars, company founder, entrepreneur, mathematician and computer scientist, dreamer, and avid boating enthusiast Andy Rebele, along with Director of Engineering Chris Gil and Principal Controls Engineer Michael Schaefer, has come up with an electric outboard he deems is the Tesla for boats.

▲ Pure Watercraft founder Andy Rebele is dedicated to finding a better way to enjoy our time out on the water while taking care of the fragile environment we hold so dear. Photo Credit: Pure Watercraft

Their company, Pure Watercraft, marked its inception in 2011 and seems to be poising itself to ride the wave of interest and enthusiasm for an alternative source of energy for boaters. In fact in April of 2016, after four years of research and testing, Pure Watercraft made an announcement that pre-orders for its first electric outboard for the market, a 40-hp/50kW model are available.

According to the company's website, the engine has been designed and built with an all-electric profile and not put

◄ With outboard power equivalent to gasoline engines of up to 40-hp, Pure Watercraft equipped boat owners can enjoy silent and environmentally friendly operation. Photo Credit: Pure Watercraft

together using parts from traditional outboards. There's a lot of information to read about concerning Pure Watercraft and I would suggest checking out what has been written so far for more insight: www.purewatercraft.com

Elco

Most likely the one that started it all, Elco is still in the business of providing electric power to its boats. Voted one of Boating Industries Best Products for 2015, the company has been in business since 1893 and has spanned generations with its innovative and often visionary work.

Long a pioneer in boat building, making vessels for private yacht owners as well as the military, Elco's foray into electrical propulsion now includes motors for inboard vessels from 15- to 85-feet in length and includes sailboats, launches, catamarans, trawlers, or any other boat that travels at hull speed.

On the outboard side, the company offers its 9.9-, 14-, or 20-hp engines, all of which are lightweight and compact. In addition, Elco offers a hybrid electrical system that

▲ Photo Credit: Elco Motoryachts

▲ An early Elco motorlaunch. Photo Credit: Elco Motoryachts

▲ An Elco inboard electric motor. Photo Credit: Elco Motoryachts

combines its non-polluting, battery-powered propulsion motors with a small diesel generator. There are even variations including having a diesel motor tied into the system as well.

According to Elco, their electric motors have an expected service life of some fifty thousand hours, are maintenance free, and of course non-polluting.

Making things even easier, the charging options include solar, shore power, wind generator, and prop regeneration: www.elcomotoryachts.com

▲ Elco's modern fleet of electric launches use the latest in alternate, clean power. Photo Credit: Elco Motoryachts

LEHR

There is a non-electric entry as well and due to its environmentally friendly profile, I decided it's appropriate to include it in this collection.

The propane-powered outboard by LEHR is as simple as it sounds. Finding propane to be a safer, more efficient and reliable fuel, Capt. Bernardo Herzer, the company's visionary and forward thinking founder and CEO, took the ideas he had put into practice aboard a North Sea research vessel into his current lineup of gas powered outboards.

Speaking with Capt. Bernardo in person is worth the admission price, so if you happen to find yourself at one of the major boat-show venues where he will be on behalf of his company, make sure you track him down.

With its vaporous nature at room temps, the propane is delivered to the combustion chamber via a patented metering system. Fueling is done in two ways with an auxiliary tank much like those usually used with gasoline outboard engines and a unique "twist and go" canister that fits into the side of the LEHR engine. The recyclable canisters are readily available at such outlets as Home Depot, Ace, and True Value stores.

With its wide range of horsepower options, LEHR offers an alternative to gasoline and electric engines: www.golehr.com

▲ Eco-friendly with zero emissions, LEHR propane powered outboards are available in 2.5, 5.0, 9.9, 15, and 25-hp models. Photo Credit: LEHR

▲ Replacing a propane canister is just a matter of twist and go. Photo Credit: LEHR

For More Information

For the latest pricing, options, new models, advancing technology, and other information on any of the companies we have discussed, please contact the manufacturers directly. Their websites are chock full of important statistics, testimonials, background and history, as well as useful video presentations among a host of other information about the exciting field of alternative energy possibilities.

There is little doubt that the shape of things to come will be providing more efficient and less polluting power for our engines, both inboard and outboard. In the case of the electric models, and with somewhat of an optimistic nod toward the aforementioned Elon Musk and others and their forward thinking work, there is still lots of engineering, thinking, and groundbreaking technology to come. But as long as the need is there, a solution will be found.

I think we should all keep a sharp weather eye on how things are progressing as the industry moves forward with this particular technology.

13. Industry Voices: What You Can Learn

"Water is the driving force in nature."
—Leonardo da Vinci, Inventor, Painter, Sculptor, Architect, Scientist, Musician, Mathematician, Writer, Anatomist, Geologist, Astronomer, Botanist, Historian, Engineer, Cartographer, and Prodigious Thinker

*I*t seems everyone has something to say when it comes to discussing anything about boats and all the stuff that goes along with being connected to the water.

So powerful is its pull, that a great many of us—yours truly included, and happily so—have made it our life's work.

With that in mind, I set out to craft this chapter of the book with some thoughts from longtime industry friends on what they think is the current state of affairs in the marine business and especially how things bode for those who are about to enter this singularly different lifestyle.

Boaters are an eclectic group, one that has as its common theme the connection we all share with the water. Yet the individuals comprising that group are as different as, well, the vast number of boats from which to choose.

I hope that this industry insight will, as everything we've discussed so far, assist you even more in making the right decision as you contemplate getting into boating.

Michael Verdon

First came to boats on Lake Macatawa, which connects to Lake Michigan and has lived in many great boating areas, including Annapolis, Cork, Ireland, Clearwater, Florida, and East Greenwich, Rhode Island. Studied American history at George Washington University and creative writing at Hollins University. He has been writing about boats and boating since 1983 and has been featured in Worth, The Robb Report, Outside, Tennis, Esquire, *and marine publications such as* Yachting, Boating, Superyacht Business, *and* Invictus.

There are significant challenges facing the industry today. They include the rising costs of new boats, more compressed leisure time, the diverse interests of younger generations who might have been the next generation of boaters and, without getting too political, an uneven distribution of wealth that makes boating seem even more expensive than it probably is.

The rising costs of boats have come partly through EPA regulations that forced engine builders to add catalysts to sterndrive and inboard engines, thus raising the cost of a boat by at least $2,000.

▲ Photo Credit: Michael Verdon

EPA emissions standards had already impacted outboard motors a decade ago, so outboard prices had their largest increases before the recession. The jump in sterndrive engine prices came at the worst possible time during the downturn, when there was already a glut of good, used boats on the market. The recession also saw new-boat buyers generally moving away from sterndrives to outboard-powered boats such as pontoon boats and saltwater fishing boats. Sterndrive unit sales have moved from a high of 72,000 in 2005 to about 13,000 last year. Many of the 72,000 new sterndrives would have been entry-level boats.

Other costs come from building in integrated "smart" technologies, mostly on the engines, that allow for joystick docking, active trim, electronic anchoring, and improved running. While many of these technologies are not on entry-level boats because of cost considerations, more are becoming standard features on outboards and sterndrives. They will push the base prices up.

Of course, the positives from the new technologies is that new boats have become easier to operate, quieter and more fuel efficient, and a lot less hassle. The builders competing for fewer buyers have really upped their game.

I won't talk much about the different interests among younger generations like Gen-Xers and Millennials, but a boating company president said his sales are now being driven by Baby Boomers, fifty-five years and older.

There are some segments, like those who pursue ski/wakeboard/wakesurf boats that are doing well with younger (under age forty) boaters, but they tend to be expensive and are not really considered entry-level models in the traditional sense. Several boat builders in this category, like Malibu and MasterCraft, have introduced value models to entice new-boat buyers who love the quality and performance.

On a positive note, the pontoon segment has returned to pre-recession sales levels. The base models are still affordable to an entry-level buyer, and they seem to have lost their "old-man" reputation as the most embarrassing boat on the lake. The manufacturers have given their lines great makeovers.

Freshwater and saltwater fishing boats have also been growing. Many of those appeal to the entry-level buyer. In the personal watercraft (PWC) segment, Sea-Doo launched its Spark model two years ago that starts around $5,000. It has done very well, pushing sales in that segment up, while more PWC expensive models have done okay, but nothing like the Spark. This proves that there is a market for entry-level boats if builders can keep prices down.

The entry-level segment seems to have found an alternative through boat clubs and Airbnb-style boat rental operations. The president of Freedom Boat Clubs told me that his business has been climbing an average of ten percent for the last fifteen years, and they're opening new branches around the country. The members pay an annual fee and can use the boats whenever they want without having to own and maintain anything. The president said about twenty-five percent of the members are new to boating, and about a quarter of those eventually buy their own boats.

There are also three or four websites that function on the asset-light Airbnb business model, renting individual owners' boats to people for a day or weekend that want to try boating without a long-term commitment. The websites claim that sales are growing each year.

Am I optimistic about the entry-level segment? Yes and no. Boating seems to be alive and healthy. The National Marine Manufacturers Association (NMMA) says that boater participation remains at all-time highs, so clearly, people are getting out on the water. But I also believe that boat and engine builders are missing opportunities at the entry level because the sport has become too expensive. In 2006, Bayliner had an 18-foot bowrider, with trailer, that retailed for $9,995. Now, that same entry-level boat starts closer to $20,000.

Boating will always be around, but I think new-boat sales will never again reach their 2006 highs because we're not getting the same sales in entry-level boats. I think it's largely due to cost, but also to less leisure time and discretionary income, especially among younger generations.

Bob Shomo Jr.

A VP at Johnson & Towers distributors for MTU diesel engines. Bob Shomo Jr. is a fourth-generation member of the company that was established by his great-grandfather, Walter Johnson Sr. and his partner, Joseph Towers in 1926. Johnson & Towers is the premier MTU/Detroit Diesel and Allison Transmissions distributor for the Maryland, New Jersey, and Delaware areas. Keeping up with rapidly advancing technological pace in both commercial and pleasure craft areas, the company has a distinguished reputation for installation and service.

I grew up in the business, starting out on the trucking side. I always wanted to migrate over to the marine side and have been on boats ever since I could stand. Having participated in fishing, tournaments, and the industry itself has really prepared me for this position.

Being on the big end of things, dealing with powerful engines that go in boats whose purpose is to go fast and travel far, usually for fishing, gives me a rather unique overview of boaters who have started with entry-level boats and worked themselves up to such vessels as, for example, the new Viking 72C.

The industry has changed a lot. Giving us improved products, especially those on the power side, one of the challenges with the design of engines is how to deal with mandatory government emission standards without sacrificing performance and efficiency and of course, cost to the customer.

▲ Photo Credit: Bob Shomo Jr.

It doesn't matter whether it's an outboard motor or a big diesel engine; it does become more complicated and will influence pricing for the end user. For example, an entry-level boater, with those complex, electronic and computer controlled engines hanging off the transom of their new boat, is not going to be able to, and but for the most basic of maintenance items, service, fix, or diagnose those motors. Therefore, you have to rely on the integrity and expertise of your engine manufacturer and its service network and make sure you partner up with the right companies. And that notion includes almost everything on that boat from electronics to any options you may order. Service is what keeps you going, whether you start out on a 17-foot bowrider or end up on that 72 Viking.

I just bought a Tidewater 25 center console boat with a pair of Yamaha 150-hp, four stroke engines and am very satisfied with having done my due diligence and the fact that hopefully, I might work my way up to a substantial sportfishing boat. Whatever and wherever this takes me, there's only one way to do it and that's the right way.

Peter Frederiksen

Lifelong boater, angler, writer for Boating *and* Yachting *magazines, columnist for* Newark Star Ledger, *freelance magazine journalist, communications manager for* Viking Yachts.

For entry-level boaters, it is imperative to attend as many boat shows as possible. In this way they can see the many models available while comparing pricing, power and electronic options, and find out why one boat might be more expensive than another.

With that comes a rather intrinsic form of knowledge. A boat is an investment of a customer's discretionary income so it's going to be a big commitment to do something like this. Along with that, the reputation of the company building the boat is going to be on the line. And the last thing anyone wants to do it to buy one from a company that is going out of business.

In the late 1980s, a lot of supposed boat builders, noting the uptick in both interest and sales, went into business by merely copying other designs and coming into the market with a "price" product. In cases like this, the entry-level boater does not have the experience and knowledge a more experienced one

▲ Photo Credit: Viking Yachts.

does. If you're going to make the commitment, get as much information as you can. Learning by hard knocks in not only a waste of time but can be a crippling economic setback. And again, attending boat shows is where to begin.

A good question to ask is why does a boat cost what it costs? While there is a pervasive attitude that just because something has the word "marine" in front of it, or in its description, that means more expensive.

Well, when you come to think of it, it's true but not because the industry wants to jack up the price of things. Look at it this way: Your boat is not a car and it is put through much more abuse, especially in saltwater operations, a very harsh environment, along with vibration, movement, and lots of bouncing around. In other words, it has to be built a certain way by people who know what they are doing to be able to handle its purpose and operation. Some good advice here is to go with the kind of company that has been in business a long time and enjoys the kind of reputation that instills confidence.

At Viking's level of design, engineering, and building, we always ask our owners where they do their boating and how they are going to use their boats. And we expect them, with our help, to always ask the right questions so they get the boat that is right for them. We want them to stay in boating and not have a bad experience, one that will keep them out of the lifestyle. I think this is important no matter what size boat you are considering.

An entry-level boater really needs to be taken by the hand and informed, educated, and given all the information before they make the decision. The last thing they need is buyer's remorse.

Sometimes they don't think about fuel capacity, warranty, layout and accommodations, the need for extra horsepower, expected resale value, and the time involved they need to have that will be dedicated to this kind of diversion and how it takes the place of what they used to do. After all, this buyer is a very important part of the industry and as they grow in experience and commitment to the lifestyle, and get sea miles in their wakes, well that can mean a bigger boat in the future.

Every day you are on the water, you learn something new and that's why it never gets old. There is nothing better than coming back to the dock and sharing stories of time spent out there, fishing, traveling, and how fortunate we are to be involved in this kind of experience.

Captain Bill Pike

Professor Emeritus of All Things Boating. Reporter and columnist for the Watertown (New York) Daily Times, *feature writer for the* St. Petersburg Times, *ship's officer on vessels plying the waters of the Great Lakes, Gulf of Mexico, Caribbean, and South and Central America. His professional certification includes*

▲ Photo Credit: Bill Pike.

an unlimited tonnage, First Class Pilot's License for the Great Lakes, and a 1,600-ton Master's License for all oceans. Captain Bill's magazine writing includes Power & Motoryacht *and* Boating. *He has received numerous awards for his journalism and has long garnered the respect of the industry.*

For me, it all started—and I would imagine it's the same thread that runs through all of us who have taken to the water—when I was quite young.

You see, my parents owned a small camp up in the Adirondack Mountains in upstate New York on a lake. We had a rowboat that was mine, and an aluminum skiff with a 45-hp outboard on it. And I could remember being out on that boat and watching the bubbles and froth in the wake and thinking this is the most fabulous thing I have done in my entire life and that I was going to continue doing it for the rest of my life as well. And I guess that's what I've done.

I've seen a lot of changes in the industry and for the entry-level boater perhaps it's a bit harder to get into this lifestyle in terms of costs. These boats are quite technologically advanced and not only in the building techniques. While all this has made, for example, docking, handling, and navigating much easier, the problem I see gets back to how much one is going to have to invest.

The market has become smaller, attracting those with lots of discretionary funds and what I would like to see is some high-end manufacturer bring into the market a boat that might not have all the bells and whistles attached to it. I mean if you look back, even fifteen years ago, there were lots of folks in boating who were just not as wealthy as others but who could still afford some kind of boat on which to enjoy some time fishing or being involved in cruising with the family. Those same people today are kind of stuck in not being able to move up because technology has made things so much more expensive.

There's a lot of good that comes out of it as well, especially on the engine side. The diesels, for example, are so much more efficient and cleaner which is good for the environment. And then there's all the work being done in not only improving what we have available now, but in alternative energy and power sources going forward.

So how does the industry self-monitor or self-adjust so that entry-level people can get in and grow into it? Boating clubs are one way I see to kind of test the waters. And there's always the brokerage market. But I still feel strongly that, and according to your needs, and if young people are going to be attracted to getting into the lifestyle, you have to provide a cruising boat they can afford. And that kind of gets back to my idea that there are boats to be had that are well crafted, have a minimum amount of equipment, and are within a reasonable and reachable economic range for someone to be comfortable with.

Right now I've got an old 28-foot Cape Dory. She's heavy and well built, with a single engine that hardly burns any fuel. She's a good running boat with a nice place to sleep, and has a galley and head. It's got a chart plotter, a radio, and a compass. And that's all it's ever going to have. Maybe I'm just a crusty old salt, but that's just me.

Andy Rebele

Based in Seattle, entrepreneur, visionary thinker, rowing enthusiast, lifelong boater, earned an MBA from MIT. Founded Pure Watercraft in 2011. The company designs and manufactures outboards and outboard battery packs for boats. Its outboards are used for fishing and leisure activities. The buzz on the company is that what Tesla is to cars, Pure Watercraft will be to boats.

There have been some rather strange coincidences in my life. I grew up in Chula Vista, California, and on weekends went fishing. I would catch crawdads and sell them to the bass fishermen.

Among other things important to a young person, I also became interested in rowing and later became a competitive enthusiast in both high school and college. And by the way, that same lake I used to fish on as a young boy? It became the U.S. National Training Center for Olympic Rowing.

Between junior high and high school, my family went to England for a year and we lived in a town called Henley, which just happened to be the headquarters of the Henley Regatta, the largest rowing race in the UK.

I was the captain of the Stanford Rowing Team, coached a girls' squad, and did the same for Boston College when I was at MIT. And whenever I went out coaching, there was the ubiquitous, outboard-powered skiff, a smelly, noisy, often unreliable 25-hp outboard chattering away as we plied the waters during our practice time.

So, here's my thought: rowing is an incredibly aesthetic sport that requires complete concentration and technique on both the competitors and their coaches. And in the middle of all this is a loud and rather foul smelling machine. It's that fragment of those days that for me, being hard-wired as I am, gave rise to Pure Watercraft.

For this next generation of new boaters, especially those not yet aboard and still considering getting into it, their profile is somewhat different.

In the past, waves of boating enthusiasm have accompanied waves of prosperity. And today, there's an incredible wealth boom in such sectors as, for example, Silicon Valley, which typically involves those who care about the environment. In fact, some sixty percent of luxury cars bought in this area are Teslas.

Enter the idea of Pure Watercraft. In 2011, I got the thought because I was already looking at an electric car, a Tesla Roadster to be exact, and asked my smartest friends for their impressions.

I looked for people who had already been involved in electric car projects and anyone who had done anything meaningful in this area. Collaboration led to our first project, a 21-foot conversion of a Cobalt boat with electric power. A year later, in 2012, we transitioned our efforts to the outboard sector.

To date, our prototype weighs ninety-two pounds, but this 26.8-hp motor delivers more than that power. When we put it on an exact hull equipped with a 35-hp traditional gasoline outboard on it, we beat it both off the line and at top speed. This is because the propeller can be so much more efficient with electric power. You see, the gasoline engine has its torque only in a very narrow rpm range whereas an electric motor has it at every rpm range. We can use a much bigger, slower turning prop at much higher efficiency with less dependency on load.

As far as battery technology is concerned, you have to treat it like a human being; it wants to be kept at a certain, comfortable level of temperature and not stressed too much in order to have a long life. We focus a lot on the thermal management of the battery pack but nothing I do is going to affect the progress rate of batteries. It will happen in its own time and I intend to be there when it does.

We have not accomplished everything we set out to do but like Tesla's Elon Musk, toward whom I have the utmost respect and admiration for what he and his company are doing, we intend to.

Right now we have prototype outboard motors we are showing around and are exceeding our own expectations. Our battery packs are doing what they are supposed to do and once we go into full production, we will be working on more advanced design and engineering making them better than they are today.

Recreational boating, for those whose needs are 40-hp and below, tenders, of course the rowing sector, people who are environmentally concerned, areas where gasoline engines are prohibited, tour operators and some work boat applications where fuel prices are a concern are those who initially will be interested.

We've invented, designed, and engineered everything, motor, motor controller, housing, propeller, battery packs and chargers, for example, from the bottom to the top. There is not one piece of this complex project that hasn't been created by us. If one thing does not work, it jeopardizes the entire mission.

Our first stage is a pilot production run including a small batch to customers who have pre-ordered our motors. Once we get that feedback, see how we handle service and operations, and as we learn, we intend to tweak the product and go into mass production soon after.

Kris Carroll

A firm believer in the American Dream, and a prime example of what hard work and perseverance can accomplish, she left her Northeast environs for those of the South, and after landing a job at a boat factory as a production clerk, spent years learning as much as she could until she became president of Grady-White Boats. Commitment to customer care is her core principle and has been a hallmark of her leadership at Grady-White.

Our company itself speaks to how connected we are to our owners. It is a very personal and important aspect as to what kind of organization we are.

We're always going to be there for them and that happens right at the beginning. In any given year, 15 to 20 percent of our customers are first-time boat buyers, so it's important we start things off in the right way. From right here at the factory, to our dealers, our service, owners' events such as Grady Fest, new and innovative programs and so much more, our commitment to excellence runs throughout. For a first time boater, owning a new or used Grady

▲ Photo Credit: Grady-White.

is a terrific way to tap into the best support system to learn all about the joys of life on the water.

For me, personally, it's been a wonderful and exciting transition from Framingham, Massachusetts, to Greenville, North Carolina. I was twenty-four years old and landed a job at a boat factory as a production control clerk. The rest is the American dream. I moved up from an administrative assistant position and then to engineering clerk and manager. Hard work, and learning all I could, resulted in a promotion to VP of Engineering. Within a couple of years, and without any formal technical background, I took over manufacturing responsibilities. And in 1993, I became president of the company. Just amazing. Likewise, for many customers, owning a boat is their dream, and all of us here work hard to make sure the boat they get gives them that exceptional experience and helps them make lifelong happy memories.

For all our owners, and especially those first timers, we just love having them come to our factory. They get a private tour, see how the boats are built, and how they work and they get to meet the people who built their boat. We all stand behind them, and that makes owning a Grady-White unique.

Our team is dedicated to delivering the ultimate boating experience and to that end, we are constantly calling, surveying, and keeping in touch with our owners. We stay focused and attentive to the issues, no matter how small. And the result is a strong, safe, feature-rich boat no matter which Grady-White model one happens to choose.

I am especially proud of our Captain Grady program, a special audio visual app feature for iPad and IPhone, that acts as your own personal owner's manual. This exclusive application is visually detailed, friendly to use, and model specific for all new Grady-Whites. It covers everything technical including startup, shutdown, troubleshooting, emergency procedures, alarms, manuals and systems including electrical, generator, load management and more, depending on the model.

Whenever a family is out on one of our boats, we want everyone to be just as comfortable as can be. Whether fishing, cruising, or out for fun on the water, that's what we're all about.

Again, another thing that is at our core, and is most important to us, is bringing in new boaters to not only the lifestyle but the family of our boat owners as well.

Whether you are a veteran boater, have a new or brokerage boat, and if it's one of ours, you have all of us with you. Factory, service, dealer. It's a complete package. We want to take care of every single person that owns a Grady-White boat. That is what makes our company special and something you get only with a Grady.

Bentley Collins

One could say that Bentley Collins went from Down Under to Down East. Originally his family was from Australia and when he was still very young, the family moved to Montreal, Canada, where Collins grew up on all things boats. From a manufacturer's agent to a sailboat dealer to a ten-year stint with Beneteau. In 1993 he joined Sabre Yachts out of Raymond, Maine, as VP of Sales & Marketing.

▲ Photo Credit: Captain Ken Kreisler.

In my opinion, the more educated a buyer is, the better, and the more likely they will be to stay in. People who come blindly into being boat owners, and just looking at a set or even a bargain monthly payment will most likely not last.

The payment for the boat is just part of the lifestyle. The actual cost that is added on can be found in the dockage, if any, the insurance, the fuel, options, equipment, maintenance, and so forth, and is critical for someone even thinking of doing this to know and more importantly, understand.

A lot of people who go to the boat shows will often see that sign reading $189 a month when in actuality it's going to be much more. And of course, depending on where you do your boating, if it's in a seasonal part of the country where the weather just won't allow you to get out, while your boating will stop with winter storage—yet another cost—those monthly payments do not.

Boating is a lifestyle choice and not an activity option and most who really commit to it, well, it becomes what you do. As far as a first boat, it's easy to say that bigger boats are more comfortable and handle better around the dock If you, for example, pick up a little 17-foot bowrider at the boat show, and once you get squared away head out on a windy day, you're just going to turn around and get back to the dock as quickly as you can. Or, even not go out at all.

On that note, the new Axius, IPS pod, and joystick systems, even for outboards, makes taking the wheel for the first time a whole lot easier than ever before. With a short learning curve, the intimidation factor is lessened and all of a sudden, boat ownership is within emotional reach of many who would never consider driving or docking one. It's that easy and I'm a big fan. In fact, if you had the money to do it, you could jump into a 40-foot boat and, with of course the proper instructional time and taking some Power Squadron courses and learning to navigate, find your comfort level very quickly. If you decide you might want to go big right out of the box, it's critical that proper training be part of the package.

With all the technology, including electronics, new building techniques, and all the other things that have driven up the costs, there are other factors in the equation as well. Look at the rising price of polyester resins, the fiberglass, the wood we build with, engines, and everything else that goes into a boat; well, all these things have gone up in costs also.

Since the recession, the number of diesel engines that have been sold has gone down significantly. This in turn makes it more difficult for those particular manufacturers to build these engines and with lower volume comes increases passed on to the end user. And I think that applies across the whole industry in terms of boat building. Someone whose production schedule saw two hundred boats a year and is now down to seeing fifty go out the door, that infrastructure cost has risen significantly as well.

Here at Sabre, we position ourselves as being situated in the mid-range in the value, luxury brand sector. We're high end but are not sitting at the top of that particular pyramid, and are semi-custom and can do the kind of tweaks and arrangements to set a particular boat apart from another. That makes the boat particularly special to its owner.

My love of boating has opened up lots of opportunities to my family and me. It's a wonderful lifestyle and I can say, even after all these years, that I feel quite lucky to be doing what I do.

Thom Dammrich

Has been president of the NMMA since 1999 and in association management since 1981. During his tenure, he launched the highly successful Discover Boating campaign, greatly expanded advocacy issues and membership, and made the organization highly important to the industry.

Most first time boaters buy very affordable pre-owned; that's almost 75 to 80 percent. If they are looking to buy new, for example, you can get one of many

▲ Photo Credit: NMMA

small boat models from a variety of manufacturers for around $30,000. And if they want to go bigger, well there's going to be a fair amount of sticker shock involved. Again, if they look in the pre-owned market, while it may not be the same boat, and won't have as many features and bells and whistles, still they will be getting more boat for the dollar.

For those getting into the lifestyle, the barriers are not that insurmountable and if you really consider your options, take your time, do your homework, and be realistic about your economics and commitment, you will most likely be able to find what you need to get started.

With new buyers, it is what they do not know that is going to be their biggest difficulty. A thorough education is essential. For the pre-owned market, it means finding a reputable broker and one they are comfortable working with, someone who understands their needs and won't push them into getting a boat that isn't a good fit. Also there's getting the proper survey by the right surveyor; this to enable them to make sure they are getting what they think they are getting and not buying a lot of problems.

For example, let's throw the ethanol issue into the conversation. Basically, this is a renewable alcohol fuel made from plants such as corn, sugar cane, or grasses. When E-10, that is 10 percent ethanol, is added to unleaded gasoline, creating the 90/10 percent mixture, and if it is introduced into a boat that has never run this mixture before, it's a problem. You will need to have all the hoses and filters switched out as well as some other things done in order to ethanol proof the boat. A buyer seeking out a boat in the brokerage or pre-owned market should always make sure the engine and fuel system is ethanol compliant before going any further in the process. No marine engine is covered under warranty to run fuels above E-10 and with E-15 being sold in many places, using such fuel can have disastrous impacts. Again, the problem for the entry-level boater here is they do not have the first idea that there is an issue with ethanol. Education is important and one should always learn as much as they can about all the issues.

I also think these kinds of first time buyers really need to understand the total costs involved to maintain and use the boat. If you're a boater in seasonal parts of the country, engine winterization is necessary as is storage. A rule of thumb, and on an annual basis, it's about 10 percent of what your purchase price was to upkeep the boat.

On another point, larger economic issues, have less effect on people who own a boat and are passionate about the lifestyle. This may be counterintuitive but for example, during the 2008 recession, new boat sales dropped 60 percent while pre-owned boat sales dropped 7 percent. People were still buying boats, just not new ones. They were looking for more value in the pre-owned market. When gasoline in Chicago was five dollars a gallon at the pump, I went out and spoke with all the yacht clubs in the area and asked if this price was going to alter boat usage during the summer time. The resounding response was absolutely not. With such a short season, there was little reason to stay off the water. Now on the other side, if you're an offshore or tournament fisherman, an upturn in fuel prices may make you cut back on your trips or even partner up with someone else, sharing time aboard. It does have an impact but not as big as many think.

If you're an entry-level boat buyer, I think it's very important to take a boating safety course, one that is hands-on; boats do not have brakes and do not operate like your car and are under such influences as wind and current. It will be money well spent.

While you don't find too many entry-level boats equipped with all the latest advances in joystick and pod design—expensive options to say the least—still, if you have the means and can make the leap, these technologies take the anxiety level way down in their ability to instill confidence in the driver.

As far as the NMMA is concerned, its importance in the industry cannot be denied. Companies, for example, get 100 percent value of their dues in just the things we do at the state and federal government levels. If there were no NMMA, they would have to create one.

My advice to the prospective boat buyer is to visit www.discoverboating. com, where we do not sell any particular brand of boat but instead, assist and help to get all the questions someone might have answered. Boating is a great lifestyle for the family to get involved in and there are lots of resources out there to help anyone interested.

Scott Croft

VP of Public Affairs, BoatUS, Scott came to the water as a young boy, water skiing with his grandfather on his 20-foot powerboat. A sailing enthusiast as well, he continued pursuing all things nautical and is currently on this third boat. He has been at BoatUS since 2002 and worked for Maritel, the ship-to-shore radiotelephone provider, which was his entry into the boating world. Before that, he was in public relations.

As I see it, one of the things that have changed over the last several years, especially for the first-time boater, is the access issue. It goes to the fact that as most boats sold in this country are trailerable, and for those who choose to launch instead of finding a marina space, just where are they going to put their boats? Some communities have covenants and restrictions on where you can

▲ Photo Credit: BoatUS

park a boat on a trailer. For those who are in this sector, they need to figure out how it's going to work for them along with the costs.

Another thing has to do with time. How much do you have to devote to this activity? With many parents working full time, new boaters look to carve out enough space within a week, and enough for family participation as well, to devote to spending a day or a weekend out on the water. While participation in boating activities is up, it is still a non-discretionary item, and totally dependent on the availability of disposable income.

New boaters have to be especially concerned about budgets and how they are going to pay for this kind of leisure activity. As we know, most boats sold here in the U.S. come from the brokerage market and this has a lot of appeal for those at the entry-level. I got my first boat, yes it was a sailboat on a trailer, for $3,000, and kept it for ten years. Of course I had to make some concessions, but it got me into the lifestyle and I've never looked back.

You don't have to spend a lot of money on boating. It can be done. According to NMMA statistics, most boating households have a combined income of $100,000 or less and in many parts of this country that is not considered wealthy. And so, the positive news is that participation is up because there are many ways to do it. It takes careful planning, both on the economic side as well as the practical side.

The challenge with new boats today is all the technology that has come our way is now packed into systems such as advanced engine design and electronics, joystick, and IPS systems. While they have made boat handling easier and far more intuitive than ever before, the cost of a new boat with all this advanced equipment can be out of reach for many thinking of getting into boating. On the other hand, I think a new boater's confidence is significantly improved with these systems. As we all know, docking is a spectator sport and anything that can take all that anxiety, dread, and unease out of bringing your boat back into the slip safely and with just the right amount of expertise and confidence, well that's a good thing. But again, you have to pay for it.

New boats are also better built and that is another factor in higher costs, one that has caused the price points to creep up because consumers want it. Boats and systems that are easier to use and have more reliability are also factors. The latest outboard engines that offer turn-the-key operations and go, the stereos and sound systems, the towing apparatus and equipment for all the water sports; all this comes at a cost to the end user. It was a lot easier when boats were a lot simpler. But here we are.

14. Gizmos, Thingamabobs, and Other Stuff You Might Want

"Fortunately the boat we rented had a motor in it. You will definitely want this feature on your sailboat too, because if you put up the sails, the boat tips way over, and you could spill your beer."

—Dave Barry, American Writer and Humorist

*N*o matter what kind of boat you have, there always seems to be something that you just have to have—some item you come across at a boat show, in your marina store, a marine surplus outlet, or a junk/nautical antiques place you may happen to discover while coming and going.

Of course, once you get it, it seems to get lost with all the other stuff you have collected. I mean did you really need that dented old diver's helmet you actually thought would make a good planter aboard? Or that worn and weathered block and tackle from an old gin pole you considered as a base for a lamp?

Well, there are some items that just might be a welcome addition to your boating experience. Here is a short list of things that can have some practical use aboard your boat. Choose wisely.

Sounds Good

The Aquatic AV Bluetooth & USB Media Player plays music wirelessly via a Bluetooth enabled Smartphone or MP3 device, or via USB connection.

A2DP Bluetooth allows wireless audio streaming and two-way communication, between Apple and Android devices and the Media Player, to view track information, songs, artists, playlists, and genres on the 3-inch color LCD display. Album artwork is available when paired via Bluetooth with Apple devices, using IAP (Information Apple Protocol) Bluetooth.

Designed, engineered, and built to withstand the most demanding conditions on the water, this rugged unit features an onboard 288W amplifier capable of powering up to 8x speakers, or a combination of speakers and subwoofers, high-quality 4V RCA (phono) pre-outs for connecting an external amplifier (AQ-AD600.4 or AQ-AD300.2) or powered subwoofer and FM/AM radio with 30x pre-set memory. Charges USB devices and devices with USB connector.

▲ Vibrant music on the go is courtesy of Aquatic AV's media player.

Compatible with most Smartphones and media devices including Samsung Galaxy and iPhone 6 Plus. And just a note here: today's marine stereo systems are specifically designed for use on the water and some are rather impressive when it comes to delivering sound. Be courteous with your levels when at an anchorage or in your dock. Or better yet, put on your earphones. www.aquaticav.com

Jump Start

I have one of these aboard my boat and it came in very handy one day when my genset would not start due to a dead battery. With a quick hook up, I had my onboard power up and running in no time.

Weego is pocket sized and capable of starting 12V batteries in cars, boats, trucks, motorcycles, snowmobiles, ATVs and more, as well as charging phones, tablets, speakers, and laptops.

Incredibly easy to use, each Weego model includes jumper cables that can be attached to the terminals of a dead battery. Easy-to-follow instructions are printed on the back of each Weego for quick reference.

To start an engine, simply connect the clamps to the battery terminals, attach the cable to the Jump Starter Battery+, turn the power on, and start the engine. A built-in LED flashlight assists in low-light situations and a strobe with SOS function (on the two larger capacity models) draws roadside or on-the-water attention if needed. A 3-in-1 USB charging cord, 8 popular-

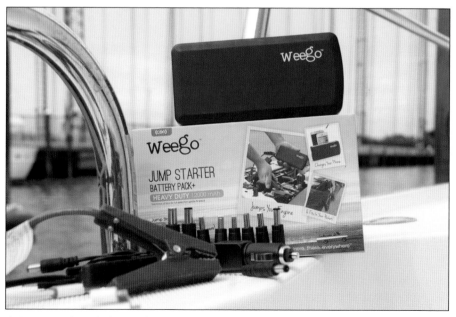

▲ Easy to use, the multi-functional Weego jump starter should be part of your boat's equipment.

brand laptop connectors, wall and car chargers, and a carrying case are included.

Weego Jump Starters are offered in three sizes. The JS6 Standard is capable of starting gas engines up to 4.6L and diesel engines up to 2.4L; the JS12 Heavy Duty model can easily start gas engines up to 6.4L and diesel engines up to 3.2L, and the JS18 Professional can start gas engines up to 9.6L and up to 4.8L diesels. Weego features built-in circuitry protection, an auto-off feature and jumper cables with both a fuse and diode to ensure user safety, as well as protection for the unit. Weego jump starters offer up to a thousand charging cycles (a full charge plus full discharge), have an operating temperature from -4 to 140-degrees Fahrenheit (-20 to 60-degrees Celsius), are independently lab tested, and are backed by a 18-month warranty from a company that's been in business for over fifty years. www.myweego.com

Outboard Auto Flush

Reverso is famed for its oil change systems, pumps, fuel primers, and fuel polishing systems.

The new Reverso Automatic Outboard Flushing System, winner of the NMMA Product Innovation Award in the Boat Care and Maintenance category at IBEX 2015, eliminates the slow, cumbersome process of manually flushing outboard engines after a day on the water.

With the push of a button, the patent-pending, permanently mounted onboard system thoroughly flushes each outboard

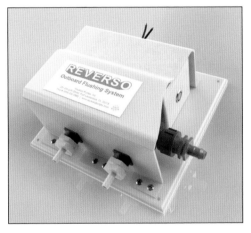

▲ Simple to operate, this handy and reliable outboard flushing system will make this necessary maintenance a breeze to perform.

engine and automatically shuts off when the flushing cycle is complete. Just one hose connection is required. This is the kind of system that makes this necessary maintenance regimen easy and quick. www.reversopumps.com

Stay Connected

The new Lifedge Ultimate Charge/Sync Cable, officially approved by Apple for use with iPhone, iPad, and iPod, has been specially designed and built to provide superior charging and data transfer performance, even under the most extreme marine conditions.

The 100 percent waterproof, extra long 2.0m (6.5 ft.) cable features Lightning and USB metal connectors that have been coated with a patented anticorrosion treatment and an ultra-tough outer coating that will never fray. A tangle-free cable carrier is included. Lifetime Lifedge guarantee. www.lifedge.co.uk

To order or for more information, call Ocean Accessories, 1-800-343-8294 (US) or email info@oceanmark.com.

▲ Keeping your bilge area clean just got a lot easier with Centek's system.

Keeping it Clean

The Centek Industries BilgeKleen filter system automatically removes oil, gas, diesel fuel, and other hydrocarbon pollutants from bilge water before it is discharged overboard.

The patented system uses a filtering medium that binds to hydrocarbons and allows water to pass through freely. As a result, over 99.9 percent of the hydrocarbon pollutants are captured, with no increase in pressure to the bilge pump. Installs easily to the bilge pump discharge line and includes an absorbent pad for the bilge sump area to capture harmful contaminants where they form.

A variety of BilgeKleen system sizes are available from Centek's worldwide dealer network to fit almost any bilge space or application, from runabouts to megayachts and commercial vessels. With one of these aboard, you'll be doing your part to help keep our waters clean. www.centekindustries.com

Ladder Sense

It happens more times than you may think. You've found a nice anchorage for the day where you can get in the water and have some fun. Or perhaps you and the family are wake board, water skier, or tube enthusiasts. Either way, getting up and out of the water and back on board usually is accomplished by using your swim ladder. And when it's time to head back home, with all the other chores one has to do, you might just forget to properly secure it.

With the Intelliboat ladder sensor on board, you'll never lose a boarding ladder again. The compact, waterproof, easy to install wireless system automatically alerts you when your boarding ladder is down to help prevent damage to it.

▲ You will never forget to bring in your swim ladder again.

Audio and visual alarms are activated when the boat ignition key is on. The system won't interfere with engine operation or with other onboard electronics. www.intelliboat.com

Avoid Fuel Spills

As a new boater, one of the most important aspects of this particular lifestyle is doing whatever we can to make sure our watery environment is protected. Whether you boat on a lake, river, or out on the ocean, when it comes time to refuel care must always be taken to make sure nothing goes overboard.

The Clean Way Fuel Fill prevents fuel from spilling out of the deck fuel fill receptacle, keeping it from splashing on you, your boat, and into the water.

The unique, baffled device works with any fuel nozzle. Just insert a Clean Way into a gas or diesel deck fill and then the fuel nozzle.

Manufactured from a clear, chemical-resistant, heavy-duty composite material, each easy to use Clean Way Fuel Fill comes with an assortment of adaptors to fit any deck fill plate and any fuel nozzle size. www.cleanwayfuelfill.com

Thoughts on Tools

And while we're on the topic of helpful things to have onboard, I'd like to discuss tools. Having a right proper tool at the ready is something that can come in handy during quick repairs or adjustments while away from the dock.

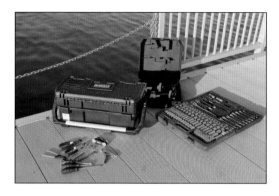

Now, you don't have to be a master mechanic to accomplish some of the things you will encounter and once you are through with your instructional period, and out there on your own, you will be picking up helpful pointers and procedures from your dockmates and fellow watery travelers.

There are some basic necessities to putting together a proper toolbox. Firstly, and for obvious reasons, get yourself a good one made of heavy-duty plastic or other non-corrosive material. If you have connections in high places, Space Shuttle tile stuff will suffice.

Levity aside, and as with whatever tools you are going to put in, go with the top brands; Stanley, Plano, Grainger, Craftsman, Pelican, and DeWalt come to mind. Make sure it's the appropriate size for your boat's needs, is preferably as airtight and waterproof as possible, and can be stowed for easy retrieval. An 18-foot bow rider does not need a rolling, eleven drawer, master mechanic's work station.

To know what you require, eyeball all the places, spaces, compartments, and work areas around your boat both inside and out including the engine room, heads, helm, and living and entertainment quarters, if so equipped. Basically anywhere these tools would be needed.

Above and beyond Archimedes's idea of the ultimate tool, *"Give me a lever long enough and a fulcrum on which to place it and I shall move the world,"* and based on the size and complexity of your boat, you need to have an assortment of flat head and Phillips screw drivers; adjustable, needle nose, channel locks, and vice-grip pliers in several sizes; nut drivers, wire cutters, spanner, crescent, and open end wrenches; a fairly inclusive socket set; a utility knife with extra blades; a tape measure; possibly a cordless drill and bits if you think this might come in handy; wire stripper; and a set of hammers—rubber, claw, and ballpeen. (All hand tools should be rubber-gripped to protect against possible electric shock, and check if you need any metric tools as well.)

Other essentials include electrical tape, duct tape, a can of WD40, ScotchBrite pads, safety glasses, multi-meter, plastic tie-wraps, hex key set, the right size batteries for all those portable electronics, a top-of-the-line Swiss

Army Knife and a suitable Leatherman tool, telescoping inspection mirror, a package of disposable gloves, filter wrench, and a rechargeable LED flashlight.

If you are away from the dock for an extended time, carry enough filters and lube and transmission oil for two complete changes. You should stock spare impellers, hose clamps, and belts and have a roll or two of self-bonding, air and watertight Atomic Tape aboard as it can provide temporary fuel and hose line repair.

I am sure there are many other useful tools you can find to help you out of a jam but this should get you started. And if there's one thing I've learned over the many years I've spent in on-the-fly repairs is to get friendly with the biggest boat in the marina; that hands-on owner or skipper usually has the best equipped engine room and the knowledge and tools to go along with it; ones that you will want in your tool box as well.

To put a dog latch on this conversation, my advice is to always be thinking on your feet and be ready to improvise and be ingenious with your tools and perhaps, anything else you can get your hands on to solve the problem and make the fix. Kind of like a nautical MacGyver if you catch my drift.

A quick P.S.: I was once working on replacing a head gasket on a six cylinder Ford Lehman diesel with a friend when I dropped a valve tappet cover down into the crankcase. After several expletives on the condition of the human experience, I then tried to figure out how to squeeze and extend my hand through the tight-fitting labyrinth of machine parts so I could get down there and retrieve the critical piece.

In a eureka moment, he looked at me and said, "Hey, how about trying that thingamabob we use when we need to get a grab on a hook that's way down in a blue fish's gut?"

I knew exactly what he was talking about.

15. Some Final Thoughts

"I yam what I yam and that's all what I yam."

—Popeye, Sailorman

"We are here to have an original relationship with the universe," contemplated Ralph Waldo Emerson, and I for one, along with innumerable others who also suffer from terminal wanderlust, truly believe that those of us who choose the watery side of that notion are well served with that preference.

When I first set out to write this book, my wish was to share with you first-time boaters the excitement, wonder, and downright fun associated with the lifestyle so, as I have, you too could also look forward to laying down your own uncharted courses. Kind of my own nautical way of paying it forward. I do hope I have achieved some of that for you.

Boating is a great way to go—to see parts of the country and the world that, being inland and on solid ground, one rarely gets to interact with. And then there are the people one meets along the way. Wonderful folks with similar feelings about being on the water that you get to share time with, swap stories or have a memorable dinner at some remote anchorage where the food just tastes a bit more savory and there is no need for idle conversation should things go quiet for a moment as everyone knows why they are here.

It's not always that way though. Breakdowns and repairs, weather, the unexpected grounding, and other factors can sometimes put a damper on things. But we get through it, sometimes using our own ingenuity and knowledge—a very satisfying feeling—but often with the help and assistance of our fellow watery travelers.

That's just barely scratching the surface. For those of you who are family boaters, you are all in for amazing experiences and ones that will form strong bonds throughout the years. I believe they are the kind that can and will add to overall positive life affirmations, allowing us to move forward in the right directions with the ability to make the right decisions at the right time.

How good can boating be? For me, it's very personal. My daughter, a recent graduate of the University of Miami's Rosenstiel School of Marine and Atmospheric Science, with her Bachelor of Science and Master of Professional Science degrees in Marine Biology with a concentration in coastal management and policy, has taken her years of boating travel and extraordinary experiences and, coupled with a concern and awareness for the world's oceans, decided to get involved with environmental issues as her life's work.

At her commencement, amid all the excitement, she took a moment, put her arms around my neck, and whispered in my ear: "Thanks, Dad."

That's how good boating can be.

I hope to see you around the docks and even better, out on the water.

Fair winds shipmates, fair winds.

Captain Ken